GREAT PIANISTS SPEAK

WITH
ADELE MARCUS

Paganiniana

ISBN 0-87666-617-9

Paganiniana Publications, Inc.
A Division of T.F.H. Publications, Inc.
Box 427 • Neptune, NJ 07753

CONTENTS

Foreword   5

The How-Why-What of Piano Playing   7

Gina Bachauer   11

Karl Ulrich Schnabel   23

Claude Frank   41

Jorge Bolet   71

Rudolf Firkusny   87

Alicia de Larrocha   107

Garrick Ohlsson   120

John Browning   144

FOREWORD

The interviews published on the pages following were under-taken at the request of Dr. Herbert R. Axelrod, the director of Paganiniana Publications and the *Musical Heritage Review.* Un-doubtedly, Dr. Axelrod invited me to write a book by and about pianists because of the duality which has characterized my career: my commitment to the concert stage and my work as a teacher of concert artists.

I was born in Kansas City, Missouri, of Russian parentage, the thirteenth child of a musical family. My early training began in Los Angeles, California, at the age of eight and a half with the Hungarian pianist Desider Josef Vecsei. I performed extensively in California both as soloist and as a two-piano team with my sister Rosamund. We were considered the *Wunderkinder* of Los Angeles. At 16, my studies continued at the Juilliard Graduate School on full scholarship with Josef Lhevinne. My composition teacher was Rubin Goldmark.

Four years later I made my New York debut as a Naumburg prize winner. This concert was acclaimed by the press "as the most auspicious debut of the season." Managers sought me for American tours, but I felt that I was too young to embark upon a serious career. I wanted to become a deeper and more knowledgeable musician.

Subsequent study for two years in Europe with Artur Schnabel and numerous appearances in recital and as a soloist with various orchestras in central Europe prepared the way for American engagements. I toured throughout the United States in recital and appeared with the orchestras of Los Angeles, San Diego, San Fran-cisco, Vancouver, Dallas, Kansas City, Detroit, Baltimore, Pittsburgh and Toronto. For seven years, I was assistant to Josef Lhevinne. In 1954, the Juilliard School invited me to join their Faculty, where I still teach.

Since 1962, I have felt the need to enlarge my musical activity. I have given Master Classes, Demonstration Lectures and Recitals in the leading universities, festivals and music conventions from coast to coast, as well as in Canada, Denmark, Norway, central Europe and Israel. Six summers were devoted to performing, teaching and giving Master Classes in Aspen, Colorado, and four summers at the Temple University Music Festival at Ambler, Pennsylvania. I am also at the present time Visiting Professor at Temple University in Philadelphia.

THE HOW-WHY-WHAT OF PIANO PLAYING

Adele Marcus

Searching for the simplest and most direct path to the understanding and study of music demands complete dedication. This quest has not only been inspiring to me as a performer, but also has helped me to guide students toward a creative handling of their potentialities.

I have evolved many theories, approaches, and practices during my life. Some of these have been discarded but many have remained in my consciousness and convictions.

The *HOW-WHY-WHAT* of piano playing may sound like a streamlined version of a highly complex subject, but when considered in detail can hardly be termed oversimplification. There is a vast difference between mechanics and technique. Technique, or the *HOW* of piano playing, not only covers a wide territory, but requires a searching intelligence for the complete utilization of mechanics and an unlimited imagination for the accurate projection of a musical idea.

Often students who practice scales, arpeggios, octaves, etc. interminably think this constitutes the sum total of technical command. Of course there is a definite keyboard approach to all these elements of piano playing, and studying them is of the utmost importance. But mechanics are only tools of an individually conceived technique.

After a thorough grounding in mechanics, we learn to understand our physical relationship to the instrument. With a genuine pianistic talent, which usually manifests itself at an early age, this necessary groundwork is comparatively straightforward. It is the way to acquire facility. However, facility is *not technique*. Very

7

often we hear extremely facile playing that sounds like "water running off a duck's back." Though this type of playing frequently indicates a drilled and super mechanism, it is often totally uncommunicative and unimaginative in the treatment of a musical phrase. A dynamic passage which requires sustained intensity and myriad nuances and color may be played in a very perfunctory manner. These additional qualities can be achieved only by a constant search into the *HOW* process!

Many musicians may feel that the *HOW* is really an interpretive gift, but I have encountered innumerable students who have definite, accurate responses to music and yet cannot express pianistically what they feel or think. This is not owing to a lack of keyboard facility, manipulation, speed, or power, but to a limited analysis of their own technique. If we cannot evolve a technique that will cover every facet of a performance, we have failed in the utilization of facility and mechanics. In the final analysis, the *HOW* means making our *own* technique!

Musicianship, or the *WHY* of our musical explorations, adds reason and authority to our study. A minute examination of the score followed by a logical questioning of all markings is a symbol of this musicianship. Musicianship must serve as the basis of all our interpretations, or the entire structure of a work loses validity and conviction.

Without a musician's grasp, a performance usually becomes a series of isolated fragments. Though perhaps technically arresting, or sporadically interesting, the work cannot stand as a solid piece of architecture. A performance must be unified in concept and plastic in contour to create an indelible impression. Musicianship, or the *WHY*, is the governor of interpretation and performance! I consider it the second step in musical study.

After we have developed an adequate physical approach and channeled our intellectual powers, we come to interpretation. Interpretation is *WHAT* we choose to convey in the recreation of a composition. This is our ultimate goal—actually our objective at all times. Whether we work with an all-embracing technique or concentrate on the composer's ideas in relation to our own responses, these considerations ultimately become the handmaidens of our interpretations. Our great responsibility is the recreation of music! This again depends upon our individual temperament. *WHAT* we

Josef Lhevinne, a supreme master of the keyboard, presented this photograph to Adele Marcus at the Juilliard School when she was studying with him on full scholarship.

9

express musically will always reveal our temperament and personality.

Tone, for example, is the most personal quality of all, and no two people possess the same tone. When I speak of tone, I mean not only the singing tone required for melodic passages, but also the general sound and texture of our playing. As some people have more or less resonance in their voice, some have more or less sonority in their sound. Tone can change during various stages in one's musical development and can be altered enormously through proper studying processes. *Listening* to ourselves with the utmost concentration is the *first* requisite for producing a singing tone.

But we must listen not only with our inner ear for what we feel, but also with our outer ear for the actual sound. We cannot possibly analyze to the last degree what constitutes a beautiful tone. It is motivated and produced by what we feel, hear, and think in addition to our keyboard approach.

Great pianists like Josef Lhevinne, Artur Schnabel, and Vladimir Horowitz (the first two having been my teachers and the last an artist with whom I've had the privilege of many stimulating talks) have strengthened my convictions about the interpreter's individuality. When someone says that we should play only what is written in the music, I am often amused. In fact, I have often said to students, "Please play what is *not* written in the music and convey to me what your imagination has dictated." We all realize that the musical concepts and interpretations of great artists are widely divergent, yet remarkably cogent.

If our temperaments are more lyrical and poetic than fiery and dynamic, or more placid and intellectual than spiritual and reflective, these qualities will be apparent in our interpretation. We may have adequate technical command and reveal sound principles of musicianship and training, but if the proper emotional ingredients are not projected, our interpretations become arid, dull, lifeless, and uncommunicative. To be able to capture and recapture the ever-elusive emotional content of any work is the acid test of the performing artist.

The *HOW-WHY-WHAT* of piano playing means applying to our studies a searching intelligence of the mind and heart combined with the greatest humility and integrity. This will satisfy every facet of our talent, knowledge, understanding, and spiritual being.

GINA BACHAUER
(Athens Greece, 1913-1978)

Gina Bachauer made her debut in Athens in 1935 under conductor Dimitri Mitropoulos. During World War II, she lived in Alexandria where she gave more than 600 concerts for the Allied Forces in the Middle East.

Until her untimely death, Bachauer, a woman of immense vitality and buoyant personality, pursued an active concert career. Her repertoire was enormous and varied; the critical acclaim for her musicianship, universal.

Marcus: I am interested to know how you view a piece of music when you first learn it. What do you actually do?

Bachauer: I have never actually started to work on a new piece of music at the piano. Perhaps this is very peculiar, but I never begin that way. I try to read it for fifteen or twenty days in bed in the evening before I ever touch a note.

M: That's very interesting. I am sure that you are one of those people who can hear through their eyes alone and totally relate to the score.

B: I like to study everything about the piece and then approach the technical problems. When I study a piece of music quietly, in bed, only my head works. I try to analyze the whole piece to see where the different themes are, and to find out what the composer's message is. After having studied this way for almost twenty days, I then go to the piano and feel that I am prepared to practice at the instrument. I understand every phrase, every tempo, where every phrase ends and the next one begins. Then, technical details, fingerings, et cetera, come later.

M: You undoubtedly establish the character, mood, and structure of all the thematic material in advance.

B: Yes. It's very strange, but this approach helps me enormously to learn a work by heart. Therefore, when I go to the piano, it is almost memorized.

M: When studying at the instrument, how do you go about your work? I realize that there are no formulas. Practicing and studying are such creative and personal processes.

B: Yes, they are. First I try, although inaccurately, to play the entire work. I want the feeling of the whole piece. Then, certainly, there are the different details to practice, how I will shape a phrase beautifully, etc. That comes later.

M: How do you practice?

B: When I have technical problems, I often practice each hand separately, because I find this helps enormously. When you are completely sure of your left hand, then you have ten fingers at work.

M: You feel that you have the harmonic structure, because it usually emanates from the bass?

B: Absolutely.

M: You then begin to experiment with different ways of phrasing, punctuation, dynamics. . .

B: Certainly, until I establish the real style and character of the music more definitely.

M: Do you incorporate the pedal with everything else at the same time?

B: In the beginning, when I want to hear what happens, I do everything together. But nothing is finished, and then I re-examine everything separately. I practice very slowly and, when I examine all the problems, I always write down my pedalings in the score, as well as all fingerings.

M: Good, I'm very happy to hear you say that. Some people do not. I personally believe in writing down fingerings for future use.

B: Certainly that will help every future generation, and especially your extraordinary fingerings. But I find that, when you finally write the fingerings down, you never change them. First of all you have to work very hard to see what fingering is the *best*. When it is written down, it is final. This is an enormous help in very difficult technical problems. When you play this piece again, you will not change the fingerings, and you will have much more security and more control in every way.

Gina Bachauer

M: After you have a clear conception of a large or small work, and it seems ready to play, you then perform it repeatedly and put it away. What do you do to restore it to your active repertoire?

B: I want to see it with new eyes completely, because the many things which have been problems become less problematical after many performances. Also, absolutely beautiful things you never saw or heard before begin to appear. I think that it is a very, very great help to every artist to allow certain pieces to sleep for a little while, and take them back sometime later. That's why artists never like their recordings. Certainly the basic things may be there, and even the big things; but we want to change details to some extent because we have changed. That's why when we hear our recordings after some years, we may want to open the window and throw ourselves out...our previous interpretation has nothing to do with the interpretation we feel now. Artists will always react in this manner. The only thing which remains the same is the technical element.

M: Because you feel firmly entrenched and secure there, with the way you play.

B: Absolutely! Then you can go back to whatever you have done, to the fingerings you have thought out and whatever else, and make changes even after you've played it hundreds of times without changing one single note or fingering.

M: I'm sure you find that the two books of Brahms' *Paganini Variations*, which you play incomparably, engender that kind of security. Even if you put them away for a long time, when your hands feel in good shape as they probably do most of the time, you can sit right down to play and feel fresh and well-practiced.

B: Oh yes.

M: But at the same time, don't you think that apropos of this subject, in order to do anything at that level, one has to constantly keep the muscles, fingers and wrists in superior condition, like one great well-tuned instrument?

B: Certainly. I have met many artists in my life with whom I have discussed this sort of thing hundreds of times. Many of my colleagues have told me, "Oh, you know, I don't need to work; I can do it without working." I don't believe it!

M: Don't you really feel that the higher your standard is, the more you work?

B: Of course, because your responsibilities are much bigger when you have arrived at a certain point of professionalism, whatever that point is, you need to ameliorate this standard every day. If you play twice in the same way, you have started to go down hill. Every day I feel *something* must improve. What this little thing is and how much better it can be is another question. But, in any case, you have to feel that every concert, every performance, everything you do, even the scale that you play every morning, even the little exercise that you do for your fingers, must improve every day. If it doesn't improve, it deteriorates. It does not remain static.

M: Ours is a very elusive art, and therefore it is not anything that is just stamped out; it is something we have to remake and recreate every single day.

With the tremendous command of the instrument that you have, and the kind of sonority you produce, do you have a technical regimen, or any pianistic exercises?

B: What I do every day is very simple, but it helps me. I think that every artist has to find out what helps him best. So many hundreds and millions of technical books have been written, but every human being and every hand is built completely differently. So you have to find exactly what suits you. What suits me is to practice simple Hanon, repeating the four notes hundreds of times, and holding the first note, so that the hand is immobilized, and the fingers work completely alone.

M: Do you believe in that more than scales?

B: Scales also. I do one or two of the Hanons, certainly in all the keys, repeating the four last notes continuously, and I do that with different colors. I start very *pianissimo* and I make an enormous crescendo and I go back to the *pianissimo* again. Then I practice them with different accents; in two, in three, in four, et cetera.

M: Even though your hand is so developed and strong, have you ever done any stretching exercises?

B: Not now. But I did stretching exercises when I was young, because I had a very small hand.

M: How many notes do you stretch?

B: When I was twelve or thirteen years old, I couldn't reach an octave. But then, at sixteen or seventeen, I could stretch to nine notes. Now, I can stretch to ten, but with difficulty.

M: That's very interesting, because it doesn't look that way; you have long fingers.

B: It looks like a big hand, but it isn't. In the beginning, I had very, very big problems with stretching. But now it is easier.

M: When you are performing regularly, how do you maintain this very large repertoire? I know that you must work many hours a day in order to do it, but how do you manage it? Do you keep everything in rotation, as it were?

B: I will tell you what helps me enormously in keeping up my repertoire. I was a very lucky woman to have three great teachers in my life. My first teacher was a Polish pianist who came to Greece. Then I worked for three years with Cortot and, for three years, I went all over the world to find Rachmaninoff, wherever he was. I would play for him and discuss music with him.

All three of these great men had absolutely the same opinion about repertoire. A young musician who wants to become a great artist one day, or who wants to have a music career, must store up music in a corner. When a student is in school, he should not work exclusively on what he will play tomorrow in a competition or recital, or possibly will play in two years, I don't know where. He must work on music that he will perhaps *never play in his life*. This music will be in reserve in a corner, and will help him when he starts a career. Then he can look at everything that he has put into cold storage, and can take out all these things that he has never played, perhaps, in public, but which he knows. I find that this is an important point that great teachers must insist upon: that young students should not just work on competition and audition material.

M: I feel this is a sad thing about the age in which we live. There are almost too many opportunities made available too soon. The temptations of a quick artistic and monetary return offered to young people through competitions, grants, et cetera, sometimes stifle their true dedication and early involvement with the learning process. We cannot blame the young. They can't resist the temptation because so many hundreds of thousands of students emerge from graduate study and never even taste a bit of a career.

B: You are absolutely right; I see the point of view of young people. However, they are catapulted onto the stage from one day to the other. The musical background is not solid enough. Then

16

they begin to work on repertoire and also to give concerts. And that's the end.

M: It's deadly. This is what I have screamed all my life to students. In fact, I've gotten into very much difficulty and trouble with them, because I feel they need longer preparation and they feel I am holding them back.

B: Because you are not *only* a teacher.

M: Also because I know what the public demands. Supposing you have three concerti that you play very well, and maybe two recital programs; how long can you survive with only that much?

B: It's impossible!

M: And when you are already in a position where you are recognized, you can't afford to sacrifice your standards. But where do you find the time to sit down and learn from scratch? Of course, I have my own ideas about competitions, and as long as we're on the subject, I think that the age limits should be changed. They should not encompass ages sixteen to thirty, but rather twenty-eight to thirty-six, because students should have a longer opportunity to develop repertoire, to prepare themselves, and also to appear before smaller audiences, thus gaining experience and security. The tremendous epidemic of "winning that prize" becomes a frantic scramble for survival. I feel like an absolute ingrate when I say this, because so many of my students have won international and national competitions. But I realize that there must be a way in which the preparation can be more substantial and extensive.

B: It has to be more extensive because, first of all, these children have to grow up, they have to go to school, they have to learn languages. An artist, years ago, who played the piano very well was sometimes a complete idiot apart from piano-playing. It's not in fashion anymore to be uninformed and poorly educated. Today, an artist is a human being with whom everybody wants to discuss not only music, but painting, sculpture, literature, everything. A young man or woman today must be completely ready for all of this. And, after learning languages, reading the classics, and finally becoming fairly educated, what about a musical background? What about harmony, orchestration, everything that makes a real musician? Today, one can't do it half-heartedly. It is out of the question. Playing the twenty-four Etudes of Chopin fast doesn't mean that you are an artist.

Youngsters have to have a solid, broad background and, certainly, a vast repertoire, because you can't concertize with a very small repertoire like Paderewski did in his time. In the old days, artists gave one concert every three months, one here and one there. They didn't have records, television, radio performances. Certainly, when they gave a concert every three months, it was absolutely perfect. If they gave a concert in Los Angeles, and then they played in New York, nobody from Los Angeles knew what had happened in New York. Well, it isn't that way anymore. Today, you must change your program almost every day.

M: Not only that, but don't you find that the audiences are so much more knowledgeable about repertoire?

B: Absolutely.

M: And the demands upon the young people are so great because they have to be able to play everything from Scarlatti to Schoenberg to Boulez to what have you.

B: Nobody can imagine how demanding it is until he experiences it.

M: In addition to talent, wouldn't you place preparation and dedication next in assuring any kind of career?

B: Yes, I would say, first talent. But you must have the *craziness* to go on continuously, whether you are sick, or you aren't sick, or you have a headache, or you don't have a headache. You must have this sort of craziness *to go on every day*. If you don't have it, success is absolutely out of the question. When I say every day, it is not only two or three hours, it is your whole life. You have to dedicate everything; if not, you cannot do it.

M: I know that you are one of the most shining examples of that fortitude and dedication.

B: Talent, for me, includes the great urge to express yourself somehow. We may encounter a young child who wants to dance, who eventually finds that this is what she must do all her life. Another child may come to you and say, "Miss Marcus, I want to learn to play the piano." There is a desire within, which has to get out. But from the moment that they say, "This is what I want to do," the agony starts. Then, at that point, how does one begin to teach something as terribly abstract as music?

M: It's abstract, and yet it isn't abstract for the really talented. Haven't you found that the very thing that motivates most students

18

is the absolute conviction that everything else is secondary? It's as though they draw creative spirit from the center of their being. This implies complete dedication. Students are nurtured by it, but at the same time, they have to nurture it; it's a two-way street.

B: But nothing else must exist. Very often when they ask me, "What makes an artist," I find that, apart from this urge to express oneself, an absolute dedication and willingness to work like I-don't-know-what, for hours without end, to build a repertoire, are the elements which are absolutely imperative. Together with all that is enormous sacrifice. I love the piano, I love music; I don't love the piano, I don't love myself, I love music. Whatever else changes, my love for music remains constant. When I heard your student play the other day, after no more than two minutes, I found that my face was completely covered with tears, because I adore music wherever I find it.

M: And you felt that was true for him too?

B: Even with all this love, it is sometimes hideously difficult to sustain. One evening I was traveling in a train from London to Manchester, and it was Christmas Eve. You know, in England, when the train goes by, you can see all the windows of the houses full of lights and Christmas trees and whole families together. I cried more bitterly on that evening than on any evening of the journey. I was completely alone in the train, and I was going to give a concert the next day. Everybody was with his family, everybody had their children and parents with them, everybody was around a Christmas tree, everybody was celebrating, and I was alone in the train; nobody else was in this blasted train. When the journey finished, I found myself in a completely empty hotel room, without anybody, waiting until the next day to go to my rehearsal at ten o'clock on Christmas Day.

M: And that is the great sacrifice.

B: But you have to do it. That is what I say to all these young-sters when they ask me "What makes a career?" This is what makes a career. If you are married, it must be your piano and your husband. If you have children, it must be your piano and your children. If you are sick, it must be your piano and yourself. Whatever you are, it must be your piano and that. If you don't put the instrument and the music that you play first, and everything else second, you will never become an artist; it's impossible.

M: I'm very happy to hear you say all of this, because we are never happier than when we have our own feelings and opinions upheld, and you've said it so beautifully. Coming from someone who has so much to give and who lives daily with music totally, the words really come alive. I think that people should realize this when they say, "I want to study, and I'm so eager to work with you, and I love music." They give love of music lip service very often, but when it comes to the real thing, they don't understand. Fortunately, there are those who really belong to the "fold."

B: That's why there are very few great artists in the world.

M: What do you feel would be the most important thing to mention concerning the strengths and weaknesses of young people in music today?

B: I would say that all young people emphasize technical problems more than musical values. I think another weakness of our young talents today is their eagerness to arrive somewhere fast. With music, you cannot do that; you pay a very, very heavy penalty for it. Every musician, every youngster, who wants to go on with music must feel the earth firmly underneath his legs. The steps must be taken slowly. To play, to give a concert or to perform in a competition—simply to appear on a stage and face the public, takes years of practice in order to gain the proper control. To walk on the stage, knowing that anything can happen to you at any moment; to know that even with what you have to give, every day becomes more difficult, is a brutal reality. Every day audiences know more, and to arrive at the piano and, in two minutes, have three thousand people in the palm of your hand, feeling the same thing, perhaps crying with you, laughing with you, and enjoying with you, is an indescribable satisfaction.

M: This takes every bit of your concentration and communication.

B: So how do you arrive at this moment? You arrive very slowly and systematically. You can't do it from one day to the other, it is absolutely impossible. This is what I find to be a great weakness in our young people today. There are unbelievable talents; I have had the opportunity to hear so many who are so great. But they want to arrive in no time at all.

M: "Instant coffee."

B: Everything must be quick, quick, quick, quick. If a young pianist, at the age of twenty-three or twenty-four, has not been completely on top of everything, he thinks he's a failure!

M: I feel that if we can get students to understand total responsibility, and how much time it takes to be thorough, and to know themselves in relation to their work, we would truly be accomplishing something.

B: It takes a lifetime.

M: Of course, it's endless. Mr. Horowitz once told me that when he was asked "How do you do that passage so beautifully?" He replied, "It's very simple; it only took me my whole life!" People don't realize that.

B: Today, the musical education and background of every young artist must be complete. If not, it's impossible to go on.

M: What do you think of students studying with an endless number of teachers? In other words they go shopping just for an interpretation.

B: If a student has had a teacher who is a total musician, he should have been thoroughly grounded. From this point he can go on alone. I think it was Casadesus who said that a young artist must stop having lessons sometime and start making his own mistakes. Because until then, he makes the mistakes of everybody he hears. He must learn to make his own, and how to correct them.

M: It is extremely important to become not only a pianist, but also a *musician* who can illuminate a score. This certainly forms the basis for their future lives.

B: And again we go back to the "storage" concept that they must learn as much as they can and store it. Never mind if they will never play it. I do not say that a young student must know all the Scarlatti sonatas; that's impossible. But if, from 600 Scarlatti sonatas he knows one, that will not help him in his life. If, however, he has gone through a great deal of Bach's music, and if he knows Haydn sonatas, and if he has done all the Mozart sonatas, and if he has read the Mozart concerti, and knows what Beethoven has written, and the Romantics, and he has examined everything from the French and Russian schools, then he has only to choose and work after that.

When I was a child, I cried my eyes out because I didn't have enough time to learn all the literature I wanted. When my professor said, "Next lesson, I would like to have the C-Minor Mozart

Concerto, the first part of the Fourth Beethoven, and the first part of a Chopin concerto," I went completely crazy, because I thought it was impossible; I could not do it! When Cortot once asked me to bring the F-Minor Concerto of Chopin from one Friday to the other and play it at his *classe d'interpretation*, I was overwhelmed. I had never played this concerto before, and I had to prepare it and play it in one week!

M: This is the kind of training I believe in.

B: But today, I am grateful, and I bless the names of my teachers continually. They killed me when I was a child, but it was right. Now, I don't have to find one Beethoven sonata or a Mozart sonata or anything else and start reading to see what is there. I may have to work, but I already know what is there.

M: Gina, God bless you. This interview has been genuinely exciting and reveals, as always, your artistic magnitude.

(Immediately following this lengthy discussion, Madame Bachauer and I proceeded to have an elegant lunch served to us in her suite at the Regency Hotel in New York. Looking back on that day, I realize even more poignantly than ever that her likes as human being and artist will not be seen again for a long, long time. *A.M.)*

KARL ULRICH SCHNABEL

Born in Berlin in the year 1909, Karl Ulrich Schnabel began his musical studies at the age of nine. His principal teacher at the State Academy was Leonid Kreutzer and he made his debut in 1926. Following that appearance came a round of recitals, broadcasts, and chamber music concerts, as well as appearances with orchestras in Germany, Austria, and England. After the second World War, he resumed his musical activities with concert tours in America, as well as Europe. He is a very active teacher today and gives master classes throughout the world, in addition to private lessons. He is the author of a book, *Modern Technique of the Pedal* which has been translated into many languages.

Marcus: My questions to you, Mr. Schnabel, will be on two levels: the first reflecting my enormous respect for your art, and the second seeking your recollections of how your father studied. In previous interviews with other artists, I have asked similar questions and have received a wide range of dissimilar answers. The individuality of each artist's interpretive procedure in study and performance has been fascinating. You may also be able to reach into the recesses of your memory and think of some invaluable and very personal comments your father made.

Schnabel: Our approaches were in many ways similar, even though I was not my father's pupil for any significant length of time. I was a student of Leonid Kreutzer.

M: When did you study with your father?

S: After working with Kreutzer, I would play for my father primarily to try out pieces prior to a performance. I know much of his teaching philosophy, but I doubt that I heard as many lessons given to others as you did when you studied with him.

M: I never realized that you had done most of your work away from his influence. I suppose he assumed—as so many great artists do—that they cannot teach their own children!

S: He always said, "In the home, one either takes the lessons too seriously or not seriously enough."

M: I know that Josef Lhevinne felt the same about his son and daughter. The daughter was exceedingly musical, but she could not stand her father's criticism. It resulted in an almost total dislike for music. This was very regrettable.

Beginning with your own way of learning a new work—what are some of your initial approaches in assembling and assimilating the material at hand?

S: It is important whether or not it is a piece which I eventually intend to play by memory. The whole system of studying is very different, depending on the desired result. For instance, if I take a piece of chamber music or a four-hand piece, I am not likely to have to memorize it. As you know, I played duo-piano for many years with my wife—we specialized in four-hand music—and we never played by heart. It is much easier to play two-piano literature from memory than it is to play four-hand works. On one piano each performer works with half-harmonies. If, however, I am studying a piece in order to memorize it, I will open the score and practice small sections from memory. Throughout my teaching career, I've found that one of the greatest problems is the fear of forgetting. Even after I have taught a student for one year, he will sometimes say, "I cannot rely upon my memory."

M: That's interesting—I haven't had that experience very often.

S: This happens constantly. I generally tell them, first of all, that they are not alone. I have found in many cases that it helps students enormously, to get rid of the picture of the score, and concentrate on the movement of the hands.

M: I feel that there are four different ways of memorizing, and if one of them doesn't come to your rescue at a weak moment, one of the others should. Of course, it's excellent to have a photographic memory—I happen to have one. But the ear plays such an important part. I never look at my hands, except for security when I am playing skips or pianistically awkward passages.

S: I also play with closed eyes most of the time.

M: Somehow the harmonic structure and thematic material are

24

I was not my father's pupil for any significant length of time. I was a student of Leonid Kreutzer ... I know much of my father's philosophy, but I doubt that I heard as many lessons given to others as you did when you studied with him ... Karl Ulrich Schnabel.

Artur Schnabel, father of Karl Ulrich, died on August 15th, 1951 in Axenstein, Switzerland from a heart ailment.

the elements I concentrate upon, almost exclusively. Learning with the music, or without, still necessitates learning musical ideas and not just notes.

S: There's no doubt about that.

M: You apparently concern yourself first, then, with the memorization. Do you read through a piece first to get an idea of the score?

S: Yes. Generally, if I were to approach a piece I didn't know at all, I couldn't study it in the way I briefly outlined.

M: One of the most fascinating things in this series of interviews has been the revelation that the approaches to this initial phase of studying a piece are tremendously varied. You can't just say to a student, "It must be done this way." It is and must be a personal and creative process. How you read through, absorb, and begin to assimilate a piece of music, whether it is structurally, harmonically, or melodically, is intensely personal. I don't begin to memorize anything immediately unless I'm pressed for time. We don't always have this pressure. But when you are more at leisure, do you usually proceed by memorizing immediately?

S: I feel that it is a faster way. I listen better if I play always from memory.

M: In other words, the visual distracts you?

S: Yes. Lately, in the last ten years, even if I am recording, I play from memory.

M: Apropos of memory, I must refer to one very interesting comment your father made after a concert in New York. He was sitting across from me at a late supper party and said to me regarding a slight memory slip he had had, "Better to forget the notes than to practice." Some people say that they like one person's wrong notes better than they like another's right notes. That little slip which your father made was infinitesimal compared with the grandeur of his entire performance.

S: He meant, of course, that one should not over-practice.

M: Did he practice very much?

S: Oh yes. He always said he didn't, but he did. Everybody says they don't, because it's a good excuse should something go wrong! Everyone has memory slips from time to time. When I was very young, I heard Rachmaninoff play. He performed his C-sharp minor *Prelude* as an encore. He not only composed this piece, but never got away from a recital without playing it, whether it was on the program or not. He probably played it more often than anything else in his repertoire. Yet he had a memory slip when I heard him play! When I heard that, I thought anything was possible and excusable, because you couldn't say that he hadn't practiced that piece enough. He couldn't possibly practice it anymore, after having played it several thousand times in public.

M: Mr. Schnabel, in fingering passages which require considerable attention, how do you work?

S: I simply try to find the best all-around fingering first. In some places it is more obvious than others. After many years of studying a piece, I sometimes will find a better fingering than had ever occurred to me before. It might happen at a lesson I'm giving to someone else. When we have two good choices it's always difficult, and we sometimes torture ourselves making a decision.

M: I did not have that difficulty, because I usually feel that you don't finger passages for the past, but for the future. In other words, even if you're moving up the instrument and back, your hand must be placed in advance so that you can negotiate the passage more easily. Speaking of fingerings, as you well know, your father had some unique fingerings, especially in his editions. When I was young, I used to wonder if he used those fingerings. I dared to ask him once, and he said very charmingly, "Don't forget, I got a lot of money for those fingerings!" But he said he didn't always use them.

S: Many of those fingerings were didactic fingerings. That is, fingerings which should force the performer to think of the music in a certain structural way.

M: That is very important. So often through the years, students have said to me, "You don't use Mr. Schnabel's fingerings, do you? I say, "It depends."

S: When my pupils ask me if they must use his fingerings, I say, "Don't use them necessarily, but study them." In studying, you may find out something about the piece which you hadn't discovered before. You might be able to think of the piece in a different way, after which you can use any fingering convenient for your hand. I do believe that different hands require different fingerings. I never force a pupil to take a certain fingering which may be wonderful for me but useless for him. I use and recom-

28

After working with Kreutzer, I would play for my father primarily to try out pieces prior to a performance. Kreutzer introduced me to technic and sound . . . Karl Ulrich Schnabel.

What one plays in public does not always depend entirely on oneself. It is often what is acceptable at the time, what is required. I have often wanted to perform contemporary works and have been turned down by those who didn't want them. . .Karl Ulrich Schnabel.

mend to my students editions which are unedited. This compels them to finger passages themselves.

M: I do too, as long as the student is advanced enough to make a good decision. Sometimes, watching students and the fingerings they use, I begin to wonder how they manage at all. I think, "It sounds better than it looks"—and close my eyes. After all, it's an aural art. I have a private student now who is 21, and he coaches singers. When I watch him play, I'm frightened! It all looks so very awkward. I say, "Do it again, and let me turn around." Then it sounds fine. I could not ever use some of his fingerings.

I once spoke to Horowitz about Byron Janis, who was a pupil of mine before he went to Horowitz. I said, "You know, when he first came to me he had ten very clumsy little fingers." He was only nine-and-a-half, of course. Horowitz said, "That's good." I found that very strange, coming from a giant pianist like Horowitz, with all of his pianistic know-how. He said, "I think sometimes when it's more difficult, they have to dig more deeply for the music." It's sometimes the same with fingerings.

S: There is an advantage in having a natural technical facility. But there is also the disadvantage, because you don't learn how to study. Some students can't rise above the level where their talent has placed them, while some who are less gifted for the instrument must go through the process of making their own technique. The latter was definitely the case with me.

M: Did you study technical things with Mr. Kreutzer?

S: Oh yes. He helped me very much. I came to him when I was 13. He introduced me to technique and sound.

M: How do you feel about the use of the pedal in Bach? I know that it's an interminable kind of a study for some people, but how do you feel about it?

S: I have written a book about pedaling. It is probably the only up-to-date book on the subject. It consists mainly of musical examples in which I have indicated possible desirable pedalings. There is not a single example from Bach in this book. Bach is so extremely controversial, beginning with the question of playing Bach on the piano at all, and continuing to the consideration of whether one should play it with any pedal, or none at all.

M: Frequently, I say that in the Baroque and Classical period, the pedal is like salt and pepper. If it isn't there, it may be too tasteless. If you have too much, you lose the music completely, and you taste only the salt. I feel that the pedal in today's contemporary music has become a real *prima donna*, it colors so much of what we do. It's so important for students to understand how to use it properly in Romantic and Impressionist music.

How do you feel about contemporary music?

S: I feel very positive about it.

M: Your father wrote so much music, yet he performed no contemporary music, except his own. I found this interesting.

S: What one plays in public does not always depend entirely on oneself. It is often a question of what is acceptable at the time, what is required. I have often wanted to perform contemporary works and have been turned down by those who didn't want them. If I do play contemporary works, I prefer to play those which are really controversial, very far out compositions which others do not yet play very often, perhaps first performances.

M: Have you composed at all?

S: Yes, but I stopped at age eighteen. I was also an avant-garde composer and performed some of my things, but I became dissatisfied with my own style after a while. Most contemporary works I have played have been those which nobody else played and in which I took an interest in the specific piece or in the composer's work in general.

M: When did you come to America?

S: 1937, for the first time, but that was only for a tour. I emigrated in 1938, and after that, I travelled a great deal between Europe and the United States.

M: But you were born in Berlin?

S: Yes.

M: Did you study with your father when you were *very* young?

S: No, I never did. My first teacher, unfortunately, was not a very positive experience. Then I went to another teacher from whom I learned a great deal, but who had to undo a lot of what I had learned from the first—my hand was much too stiff, and so on. Then, after these two teachers, I went to Leonid Kreutzer.

M: In one of your father's classes, he said that he did not play much Bach. Do you know why?

S: I'm not sure. His repertoire was not nearly as limited in early times as it was during the last twenty years of his life. In his later

It is important (when learning a new work) whether or not it is a piece which I eventually intend to play by memory. The whole system of studying is very different, depending on the desired result. For instance, if I take a piece of chamber music or a four-hand piece, I am not likely to have to memorize it. . .Karl Ulrich Schnabel.

years, he played Mozart, Beethoven, Schubert, Schumann, and some Brahms almost exclusively, with a smattering of Bach and Weber. In his earlier career, he played the Liszt *B-minor Sonata* a great deal, several pieces of Chopin, and some contemporary pieces.

M: What I find so phenomenal is that his Schubert was so great, and yet he was renowned as the greatest Beethoven specialist.

S: He resented this, of course. He didn't want to be labeled so specifically. He wanted to do more Mozart and Schubert after he began recording, but he was already stamped as a Beethoven pianist. He fought all his life for his belief that the composer is more important than the interpreter. He felt that one must follow the text and the indications of the composer. He believed in using the most accurate editions, only those which represented most precisely the scoring of the composer. In the early times, this was an almost hopeless fight. He was considered pedantic and schoolmasterish because, at that time, everyone played exactly as they pleased, disregarding the composer's instructions and intentions. It was mainly Toscanini and my father who were fighting for these concepts. It is hard for young people to realize the extent of this fight, but they were finally victorious—at least for works of Mozart, Beethoven, and, to a certain extent, Schubert. The battle was not yet won for works of Schumann and Chopin, which is very peculiar, because Beethoven has comparatively few indications in his text. One should, therefore, have more freedom in playing Beethoven than, for instance, Schumann or Chopin, who have so many more markings. The strange thing is that even now, the more indications there are in the music, the more they are changed by lots of performers. They do very much as they please, even to the extent of dramatically altering dynamic or tempo markings. This is in great contrast to their classical playing, which I find overly strict and confined. This is only one side of it. There was another side about which my father frequently spoke. In many interviews and musical talks, the question always arose: "What is it that *creates beauty* in a musical performance?" Answers to this question are often avoided by many people. My father fought for the belief that the beauty in a performance *is created by its proportion.* By its minute proportions—melodic, harmonic, dynamic, rhythmic, structural proportions. These minute differences be-

34

tween voices, between the different notes within a voice, between the different values of a bar, these things seem to create beauty more than anything else. This was, at least, what he so very strongly believed in, what he constantly taught, and what we try to follow.

M: This reminds me that Goethe said that proportion is the greatest thing in art. Of course, it's the greatest thing in everything, in life itself.

S: In all art. Music has architectural elements just as much as architecture itself, or painting, or sculpture. In my opinion, it is these elements of proportion which we ought to stress in teaching.

M: I agree with you so much. You have expressed this very important concept so interestingly. You spoke first about what beauty is. All of the things which you mentioned, such as the emotion, feeling and character of the music, can be cold and meaningless if the proportions are not correct.

S: It can be cold, but as we know from the other arts, there can be great cold beauty. We know this from the pictorial arts. We have it in music too. Something can be, on the one hand, enormously emotional, and practically overheated, and yet not beautiful at all because it is badly proportioned.

M: We're speaking, then, primarily of what beauty is, and not what it emanates from. But don't you feel that if one overly intellectualizes about all the things that you mentioned—the proportion of sound, tempi, dynamics, or whatever—without any inner feeling, the result can be a very frighteningly cold product?

S: Absolutely. But matters of proportion are not only intellectual. Very often, our instinct will tell us about a proportion. But if we don't know about it, then we may be lost.

M: Right—that is beauty. It is very difficult to deal with the two extremes in students. Those who feel that they overwhelm an idea with too much emotion, and they therefore suffocate it, and it loses its value entirely. You can stifle an idea with too much emotion. But when there is not enough, you have a totally cold product.

S: Of course. Without emotion or feeling, there is no greatness in music.

M: Your father taught me the meaning of musicianship. You are a musician if you can reason. You don't have to be reasonable, but you have to be able to reason, everything on the printed sheet. This

Music has architectural elements just as much as architecture itself, or painting, or sculpture. In my opinion, it is these elements of proportion which we ought to stress in teaching. . .Karl Ulrich Schnabel.

is what your father put me on the track of for the first time in my life. I didn't understand it in the beginning but I knew how great it was. It was as though he opened up the Bible for me.

S: I'd like to speak a little more about this world of emotions which we performers have to reproduce to such a great extent. Only musicians, actors, and dancers, practically no others, have to reproduce emotions in this same form. Others, like painters, do not at a certain moment have to reproduce an emotion. This is often very important in making clear to oneself, "What can I do to reproduce a certain emotion at a certain moment, if I don't feel that way at that time?"

M: That's the acid test of a great artist.

S: What do we do when we come up to a platform and we feel extremely happy, but we have to play a tragic piece? How can we at that moment play and picture something tragic if in our own center of being this feeling is not there at all? I have come to a conclusion which I think concerns all performers very much. How do we develop this ability that, if in bar 39 there is written *appassionato*, we are able to feel passionate at that moment, in a fraction of a second, that we can get any feeling out of ourselves at any time when it is needed? I have talked to very many performers about this. We have always come to the same kind of solution, namely that what we as performers do in our lives is in contrast to other human beings. Whenever we experience emotions, by going to a museum, a concert, by being in a particularly beautiful landscape, or in a life situation which brings about very strong emotions, we immediately store away these emotions somewhere inside, put them away, and say to ourselves that we will save these emotions for another time. We eventually develop an enormous system inside which is like a giant parking garage or an enormous storage place, and in each one of those little boxes there is a different emotion with a closed door in front of it. When we come to a place in the music where it says *agitato*, where we need agitation, we open the door marked "agitation" and the feeling comes out. If we open the door a little bit, we have *poco agitato*. If we open it all the way, we have *molto agitato*! We can get any kind of expression by just opening the right door. If it weren't for this ability, we couldn't do it. We cannot go through all those associations again. If we have, at the moment when we need the *agitato*, to think about a situation in our life when we were agitated, by that time we are already half a page further in the piece, at a place where it says *tranquillo*. Then finally, and at the wrong time, the agitation comes out!

M: This is very interesting. But I really think that musicians are blessed with a tremendous imagination, otherwise they would not want to sit at a thing called a piano with black and white keys and pour everything out into this. As Horowitz once said to me, it's so abnormal to try to be expressive through this thing called an instrument and bring human emotions to it, but I think we do it because we live in our imaginations. You can imagine something immediately *agitato* or *tranquillo*. But however you imagine it, one thing is certain: if you *don't* imagine it, then nothing that you play is going to come to life. With regard to storing up experiences, what about the enormously gifted child who spontaneously reacts to the right emotion of the music? He has *not* had time to store up any experiences!

S: But we have to have it ready somewhere where we can release it at any moment.

M: When a painter puts something down on a canvas and looks at it after one or two years, it's still there. On the other hand, all of our reactions have been formulated in advance to such an extent that we are like actors who are called upon to play different roles. We are *re-creative* people.

S: Yes, we have very much in common with actors.

M: Absolutely. I feel that this is the test of any artist, to be able to conjure up that very set of reactions. This is why we practice and study, and all of those proportions that we spoke about come to our rescue, to make it logical, plausible and coherent. It is not what we do to the music, it is what the music does to us, that we want to reveal.

In this photograph Mr. Schnabel is demonstrating for the author his vibrato idea on a chordal pattern with the use of the pedal.

S: There are always two sides to any art. The emotional content and the form. One without the other is nothing. For the former you need the emotions; if you don't have them you will never be an artist. If you are a performing musician, you have also to be able to muster any one of these emotions instantaneously. I think it helpful to know where they come from. Too many people are unaware of where they get their emotions. They don't know that they have a whole inner system from which they can conjure them up at any time. But however many emotions we have, we also need to put these emotions into a form. And for that form, we need to understand the proportions.

Without emotion or feeling, there is no greatness in music . . . Karl Ulrich Schnabel.

CLAUDE FRANK

Claude Frank made his debut with Leonard Bernstein and the New York Philharmonic in 1959. Since then, he has toured extensively in Europe and the Americas—North and South. Frank spent his early years in Nuremberg, Brussels, and Paris. World War II cut short his studies at the Conservatoire and forced the young pianist to flee on foot with his mother across the Pyrenees. When he finally came to the United States, he studied piano with Artur Schnabel and conducting with Serge Koussevitsky. He is married to the fine pianist Lillian Kallir, and lives in New York.

Marcus: When you first view a totally new piece of music, how do you go about learning to play it?

Frank: At my age, the occasions are becoming rarer and rarer when I am called upon to learn something completely new. The only completely new music is contemporary pieces just written, or those with which I am unfamiliar. At this stage of my professional life, this does not take up the bulk of my activities.

M: I understand that perfectly. But, as you well know, the crux of most students' difficulties is that they don't know how to go about their work properly. In their studies, students often fail to ascertain the shape of a given work, the outline or structural meaning. What do you suggest, individually, as a valid formula for study? Everyone, of course, has his own way in these matters, but what, in the main, is your personal approach?

F: The most important thing, to me, is not to be rigid about anything. I believe neither that one has to work away from the piano nor that one must always work at the piano. I personally prefer

to study at the piano for the simple reason that the sound is there. Music is composed of sound, so why eliminate the most important aspect of the music which is ever-present? Needless to say, in one's professional life there are always emergencies and extraordinary circumstances when one must learn something very quickly, or has to decide upon a program or approve a concerto at short notice. At such times, whether on a plane or train, one can begin to study a work away from the piano. This can be very satisfactory, even very exciting at times. These circumstances aside, I prefer to study at the instrument.

M: Would you, for example, begin by reading through an entire section of a large work to grasp the scope of the music, or would you proceed more slowly?

F: Definitely the former. If the work in question is large and contains several movements, I would always look through the entire piece first. I would read all the way through, no matter how inadequate it might sound or how much I might have to fake.

M: Even if you were already familiar with the work, you would still choose to finger your way through it?

F: Yes. I want to be familiar with the work not only in a theoretical and acoustical way, but also in a physical way. This is why I study at the instrument. The physical rapport with a piece is a very important element in developing a satisfactory interpretation. Therefore, my first approach is simply to read through the work unworriedly and to fall in love with the music, all the while contributing the additional dimensions of my own response to the piece.

M: Then what do you do? Do you work with an isolated passage or thematic material? How do you work after you have established an initial rapport with the music?

At my age, the occasions are becoming rarer and rarer when I am called upon to learn something completely new. The only completely new music is contemporary pieces just written, or those with which I am unfamiliar. At this stage of my professional life, this does not take up the bulk of my activities. . .Claude Frank.

F: At the risk of sounding negative, let me tell you first what I *don't* do! I do not, when learning a work, seek out the most difficult passages and practice them first. My reason for this is very basic. Very often, one's musical appreciation of the architecture and the beauty of a piece helps one over technical hurdles. Schnabel was very categoric about this matter. He, who made a tremendous impression upon almost any musician, once said "Technique will never produce music; music will sometimes produce technique." I think this is perhaps a little too strict. Music will more often than not produce technique; it nearly always does. Technique, on the other hand, may not produce music, but a fine technique in someone who is already very musical can only serve to enhance the music message—this can be very illuminating.

M: Not only that, but it enlarges the range of interpretive possibilities, comparable to having a large vocabulary in order to express yourself as eloquently as possible. One can speak very simply and seem very interesting or charming, but there are also times when one desires nuances in speech to bring out subtleties of meaning. For me, this is one advantage of having a highly developed command of the instrument.

Claude Frank photographed at age 16 during a special broadcast to Germany from America while we were still at war with Germany—from which country he and his parents had fled.

F: Our point of departure was difficult passages in a new piece. In this area, my own experience has borne out another of Schnabel's statements: "No one gets up at six o'clock in the morning to do nothing, but one might gladly get up at five o'clock in order to do something exciting." Therefore, when something musical is at stake, the necessary part of one's technical equipment is already helped by that which makes musical sense, which has a feeling of musical urgency. The gist of my reason for not isolating difficult passages when first learning a piece lies in this concept. Sometimes when studying a piece I come to a passage which is technically difficult, but if I play from the beginning, being aware of what comes next, the passage seems so predictable and so musically obvious that part of the necessary technique can come from that.

M: I agree with you one hundred percent. I think young students should hear these things, and yet all of us have sometimes awakened at five in the morning realizing that an awkward chordal or octave passage was a threatening technical hazard. It may not be exciting but it is a necessary evil to conquer. However, during my many years of teaching, students have often come in for a lesson and said, "I started with the last movement, because I wanted to get it done and out of the way." I absolutely hit the ceiling!

F: Of course, there is a practical, pragmatic reason for this. Students think that it's going to take longer to learn these passages and they want to finish everything at the same time. That's much too practical. So often, someone tells me he is studying Op. 110 of Beethoven, and that he is beginning with the Trio of the Scherzo because it's very fast. This approach is totally wrong, in my opinion.

M: The difficult passages seem to constitute the whole sonata in the minds of many people. If they can play them, then they feel justified in learning the rest of the piece. How often a pupil has said, "The skips in the second movement of the Schumann *Fantasie* don't disturb me."

F: This is idealistically wrong, but even from a practical point of view it's still wrong for the reason I mentioned before. For example, if you have learned the first movement of Op. 110, then you already have the musical basis for the Trio of the *Scherzo*. This is the positive reason why I'm against this other approach. The

46

I do not, when learning a work, seek out the most difficult passages and practice them first. . .one's musical appreciation of the architecture and the beauty of a piece helps one over technical hurdles. . .Claude Frank.

47

negative reason is that it is psychologically very bad for you; you can set up traps for yourself—psychological hurdles. When you know the whole piece and you come to the place you've worried about all the time, then you're really worried! This is a performance problem. However, there are two exceptions to this rule about not learning difficult passages first: when I restudy a piece for the thirtieth, tenth, or even the second time, I will sometimes proceed this way. I remember that certain passages take more time, physically speaking.

M: Don't you also feel that, when you're on tour with a number of programs to perform and haven't much time, you go to certain passages which feel awkward and try repeatedly to solidify them? These problems may be musical and technical. Sometimes to put music into the most technically demanding sections is the biggest challenge.

F: There is one other exception to my otherwise rather rigorous rule about not isolating difficult passages first: when the technical problems are not nervous problems like those in Op. 110 or Op. 81a, but are purely muscular, physical things like a trill, or an octave passage. For example, the trills at the end of Op. 111. I feel that there is no harm in practicing trills a great deal at the same time that one is practicing Op. 111. This, to me, is not isolating a passage. I know that when I approached the *Wanderer Fantasy* for the very first time, I practiced more octaves than I had previously. I even practiced the octaves in the piece, because this is not a nervous difficulty, but rather an endurance problem.

M: Horowitz once told me that as many times as he played the Sixth *Hungarian Rhapsody*, which after a number of years has become almost banal to everyone but is still a good piece, he had to go into training for three months in order to be able to play it with the necessary lightness, speed, nuance, and color, and not feel as though his arm was going to fall off if he wanted to make a crescendo. Horowitz, who has such phenomenal octaves anyway, had to practice octaves very slowly in order to gain endurance. Josef Lhevinne, who was a pianistic wizard, always advised practicing everything at four different tempi. First, very slowly for total stretching of the muscles. Then a little faster, which is very hard to maintain. Then still faster. Then, find the most uncomfortable tempo, and stick to it until it becomes comfortable. It is usually

48

Personally, I prefer to play more on the cushions of the fingers, rather than with curved fingers . . . Adele Marcus. I, on the other hand, play mostly with curved fingers. There are times, of course, when our approaches would overlap . . . Claude Frank.

easy to play anything very slowly and sound accurate. By the same token, it is sometimes very easy to play terribly fast. But it is the moderated tempo that often presents a problem. Therefore, Lhevinne advised four tempi for things that were shaky, even things he himself already knew. Don't you feel that, once you've played a piece very fast, it is very hard to return to a slower tempo, because the faster tempo simply feels good?

F: *There is absolutely no substitute for slow practice.* Let me embellish this by saying that, ninety-nine times out of one hundred, this slow practice should be very musical. There are very few instances in which slow mechanical practice is beneficial. Musical slow practicing is the key.

M: With every nuance, phrase, slur, legato, staccato, and pedal in place.

F: This kind of practicing is the best for everything. It's best for technique, security, nerves, memory, and everything else. Most things which one knows slowly, one also knows well.

M: But if you play too much this way, don't you feel there is a danger of sometimes losing the courage for high speed and bravura?

F: I have come to the conclusion that everything is equally difficult, if not for one reason, then for another. I've talked to many people about this who think things through very thoroughly, and I've had the answer, "Yes, but is it not true that when you're in an accompanying position, things are easier? Doesn't a second violin have an easier part than a first violin?" This just isn't so. The burdens of a second violin in string quartet are tremendous. The responsibilities of an accompanist are tremendous. They may be different, but they are no less difficult. I once had the opportunity to perform Mozart's K. 1 in Philharmonic Hall. It wasn't the fact that the concert was in Philharmonic Hall that made the performance difficult, but it was the unique responsibility of playing the first minuet that Mozart wrote.

I once played the **Funeral March** *from Beethoven's Op. 26 for Schnabel. It was a bad lesson to begin with, one of those days when I couldn't do anything right for him. . .Claude Frank.*

M: Many students, even those who presume themselves to be at the artist level, do not realize when they see a few notes on the page that this exposes them more than a lot of notes do. In the case of very few notes, the interpreter really has to have quality, and must really have something to say. A great artist once said to me, "There are only two reasons to be nervous: one is that you are not properly prepared, the other is that you have nothing to say."

Do you do a great deal of teaching?

F: I do very little private teaching of individual students, but I hold a great many master classes.

M: When you are advising someone about repertoire, do you advise young students against studying and performing very advanced works which look very impressive on paper? I often tell students that Beethoven did not start with Op. 111, and it would be better to study a much earlier sonata in order to understand his style and way with music.

F: They have to earn the right to study the later works. I think it's almost immoral for a young person who has played perhaps one or two Beethoven *Sonatas* to play Op. 111.

M: When I was growing up, nobody could play a late Beethoven sonata in public. I studied Op. 106 when I was thirteen and a half years old. I studied Op. 101, 110, and 111 when I was also quite young. But when I played publicly, I would play the earlier sonatas, up to Op. 90. Today, many young pianists feel that the early sonatas are somehow beneath their dignity!

F: This is very dangerous from all points of view. I became disturbed when some musicians remark that fifty to a hundred years from now, the only Beethoven Sonatas that will interest people will be the late ones. I couldn't disagree more. This is a very prevalent attitude about all "old" music. Undoubtedly young people still think that if they program the later works, the public will assume they are more mature. The contrary, however, is usually true.

M: They think that it looks well on paper, but after all, music is an aural, not a visual, art.

I'd like to ask you about your experience with young pianists who rarely use the left pedal. Have you taught students who are loath to play the left pedal, who think it's a cardinal sin? I assure them that they are merely playing on two strings instead of three; nothing extraordinary is happening!

F: I usually find that when the left pedal is conscientiously ignored, some teacher has written in the music, *No U.C.,*[1] or *T.C.*[2] at all times. This is shocking! I don't always practice what I preach where the left pedal is concerned. What I preach is quite opposed to what Rubinstein once said on a television interview, which was the he always uses the left pedal, even in forte passages.

M: Pianos today are very brilliant, and tuned a little on the high side. In some music, I feel that if I don't use the left pedal, the forte will be blatant. I would rather give more in sonority and produce a more veiled forte sound.

F: You're coming very close to my own idea. Let me first give you someone else's opinion who, although a tremendous admirer of Rubinstein, is diametrically opposed to him as far as the left pedal is concerned: Eugene Istomin. He uses the left pedal very, very sparingly. He says, "Don't use the left pedal! If you do, you'll sound like a hundred other pianists who use the left pedal!" What he meant rather humorously was that you may lose your individuality of tone if you use the left pedal.

M: I don't feel that way.

F: My own view is that the left pedal does give the sound a certain characteristic quality in most cases, even though it's only a question of reducing the number of strings. It's not so much the quantity of sound, but rather the quality, the kind of sound you wish to produce. That is to say, there are instances of pianissimo played without the left pedal, and there are also instances of mezzo forte or even forte played with left pedal.

M: Certainly. I think that even the very talented student needs to arrive at the point where he uses the pedals just as easily and as discriminately as he uses his fingers. The pedals can and must be used in all combinations. When you feel that something doesn't sound intense enough, you should almost inadvertently release the left pedal, even in a pianissimo passage, because you want a sound with substance which will project. A possible exception might be a piece like the *Berceuse* of Chopin, which can sound more or less uniform with little inflection. Unfortunately, I find that many

---

[1] *Una corda* = left pedal.

[2] *Tutte le corde* = all the strings, a term indicating the release of the left pedal.

young pianists regard the left pedal as their mortal enemy. I ask them, "Why do you think it's there in the first place?" I'm sure you feel that pedaling is a very great art, and that it is not treated imaginatively enough. It's like salt and pepper; if you have too much, you kill the taste—if you don't have enough, it doesn't taste at all. Taste, however, is so individual. Therefore, pedaling is a most subtle ingredient. Mr. Lhevinne used to say that pedal is the soul of the instrument. To me, that is a little exaggerated. On the other hand, there have been times when I felt that it was the soul, because it was so obviously missing.

F: I have noticed, in hearing and speaking with young people, that very often they don't realize there is such a thing as an instrumental pedal which does not make notes sound together, but which can color each note. Using it is a great art. My wife (*Lillian Kallir, also a gifted pianist* **M.**) and I differ a little in these matters, and this is one of the main reasons why we don't play more four-hand literature at one piano where one person must pedal for both. Basically, Lillian uses more pedal than I do.

M: When Mr. and Mrs. Lhevinne would finish a recital together on two pianos, Rosina would say, "Thank God, Josef, you used my pedal." He would reply, "How can you say such a thing? It was my pedal used!"

F: Did one of them habitually use more pedal than the other?

M: Mr. Lhevinne was a genius with the pedal. Mrs. Lhevinne generally liked it a little drier. He played in such a way that he could start *ppppp* and reach mezzo forte in what sounded like a big crescendo. In the most intricate passages, he would produce a magnificent mosaic in sound, with millions of fleeting nuances. The color was wonderful. His recordings do not reproduce this magic as it projected itself in the hall. For example, his *Feux Follets* of Liszt was inimitable. When sitting in Carnegie Hall you would have sworn that a bee was buzzing in your ear. It was also the absolute manipulation of the pedal. Suddenly he would open into a big ravishing crescendo, but not one note was ever blurred.

F: Speaking of pedal, there is another thing that neophytes often don't realize: the *absence* of pedal is as much a part of the art of pedaling as the *presence* of pedal. Very often, when playing with orchestra, you have to take the pedal away in order to cut through orchestral sound. To the untrained, pedal means loud and no pedal means soft. Not true! I've heard string players say to me or to other pianists who play with them, "It's too loud, take off the pedal." Very often the balance is much better with the pedal on, because the sound is not as incisive.

M: There is also the question of using pedal properly with certain staccatos; sometimes this is desirable.

F: I once played the *Funeral March* from Beethoven's Op. 26 for Schnabel. It was a bad lesson to begin with, one of those days when I couldn't do anything right for him. We came to the beginning of the *March* and he thought it was too fast, and that I should put the pedal down at the beginning. By that time I was already a little rattled and I said, "Mr. Schnabel, what about the dots on the notes?" (I was only a little boy then.) He went to his piano and played a staccato arpeggio in C major with the pedal all the way down, making it sound staccato.

M: It disturbs me when students reach a climactic point and suddenly play staccatos; they lose the total meaning by becoming too literal-minded.

F: First of all, a staccato does not necessarily mean a terribly short note. It means that the note is *detached* from the next note. Sometimes it's a rhythmic articulation. One can play a short note with pedal, and it will sound different than without pedal.

M: I finger-pedal Bach and even Mozart a great deal.

F: I finger-pedal practically everything. One of my favorite slogans is "Legato is the soul of piano-playing." But the important commitment is to do it with the hands.

M: In any accompaniment, whether it's Brahms, Schubert, or even Mozart, I hold down one or several notes of the predominantly underlying harmony; then the pedal is not necessary.

F: The life in the accompaniment is very important. If you pedal it all the way through, you take the life out. If you don't pedal at all, it gets dry.

M: Please tell us something about how you memorize.

F: I have a freak memory. Without bragging, I can say that fifteen years from now, I will be able to tell you exactly what you said to me this afternoon.

M: I only remember the interesting things!

F: Unfortunately, I remember everything—I can't shut anything out. This includes music. Therefore, I've never had to consciously memorize anything, unless I am under pressure. Without public pressure, I could play for you most of the things I've ever studied. This has advantages and disadvantages.

M: Do you have perfect pitch?

F: No, I have perfect pitch only from music to ear. If I hear something on the radio or piano, I will not go wrong. But if you ask me right now to sing a pitch, I can't do it automatically. One way is totally reliable; the other is totally unreliable. As far as my memory is concerned, it goes beyond music—it's a total recall situation which functions for me when I am not under pressure. With pressure, it disappears. By the time I have practiced something thoroughly, and there's always a reason to practice, either a technical passage or just for the joy of playing it, I know it from memory.

M: But you think harmonically, don't you?

F: Yes. However, I do know what the memorizing process is all about because I have discussed it with many other people and with students. I usually talk about the process of memorization as a four-fold thing. It is partly acoustical, partly mechanical, partly visual, and partly intellectual.

M: I name it differently. I have always had a photographic memory. If I went into your home and glanced at your living room, I could walk out and describe everything in it. This was the way I memorized before I studied harmony. I use the ear and the tactile sense, but I think almost totally harmonically. However, I listen melodically. Those are my four ways.

F: What I call the intellectual aspect of memorization is a kind of "public" memory to remind oneself, for example, "Here it comes for the third time." This is different from the other three elements.

M: That is a structural as well as a musical thing, since there is usually a musical reason for a passage being repeated for a third time.

F: I am different from you and my wife in that I cannot describe anything *visually* after I've seen it, unless I make a special point of saying it in order to remember it. This, then, becomes an acoustical memory which stands me sometimes in very bad stead when I do not recognize someone whom I have recently met—only when I get to know more about the person can I remember.

I do know what the memorizing process is all about because I have discussed it with many other people and with students. I usually talk about the process of memorization as a four-fold thing. It is partly acoustical, partly mechanical, partly visual, and partly intellectual. . .Claude Frank.

Sometimes I feel that the absence of visual recognition has sharpened the acuity of my other memory faculties.

M: I know some very good pianists who must look at their hands to play. I don't. From the very beginning of my musical experiences, I closed my eyes whenever I played a melody. I played almost exclusively with my eyes closed without being aware of it. This included the most difficult passages. A lady who heard me play at the age of eleven said, "Do you know that you play with your eyes closed?" I started to cry, because I thought I had some kind of disease! I went home and asked my sister if I played with my eyes closed. She said, "Yes, but what difference does it make?" The next day, I tried to play with my eyes wide open and couldn't. I didn't feel anything—totally detached emotionally. This disturbed me for a very long time until I heard Pablo Casals at Town Hall when I was sixteen years old. He walked on stage with his cello, sat down, and closed his eyes. I thought, "Thank God, somebody else does it too." Mr. Lhevinne never mentioned it to me. However, he once asked me to play *Feux Follets* with my eyes closed; I did it without missing a note.

F: This is mostly a matter of tactile memory. I can play even difficult things if the lights go out.

M: I love to practice almost in the dark, with only a very dim light. I feel that I can hear better.

F: In spite of the fact that I have no visual memory at all, I have a God-given freak memory in every other respect, musically speaking. There is another instance, outside of not recognizing people, in which the lack of visual memory serves me poorly where music is concerned. I do not memorize music easily that I do not hear thoroughly. For example, some contemporary music. I can force myself to memorize, but it's hard work, and I tend to forget easily.

I love to practice in the dark, with only a very dim light. I feel that I can hear better. . .Adele Marcus.

M: I can give some students Schoenberg, Webern, Elliott Carter, or something totally avant-garde, and they will bring it completely memorized in one lesson. By contrast, a Mozart sonata in the same length of time will result in one movement barely learned. These students are devoid of any emotional identification with the music, but the moment the mind begins to work like a trip-hammer, they get the patterns into the fingers quickly. Often this is where they feel most comfortable. Personally I memorize all music very fast. I learned a little bit from Stravinsky while traveling with him, playing his *Concerto for Two Pianos*. We had ten days to prepare it, and I said, "Will you play the Concerto *auswendig*?" He exclaimed, "My God, no! I could never memorize it!" The tactile finger patterns are very important for me. If the fingering is secure, everything feels comfortable. Approximate tonalities also help to some extent. There are certain things in the music which say to me, "This is what I attach myself to."

F: I call those my gas stations. I memorize contemporary pieces in much the same way. Mostly tactile and a little of the intellectual.

M: Do you do any kind of technical procedure?

F: This is a subject in which I'm very interested, because I've studied under so many different influences. Opinions differ very widely in these matters. One's own opinion changes also from time to time, depending upon one's influences. When I was very much under Schnabel's influence, I did not work at many abstract exercises, because he didn't believe in them; in fact, he laughed at them!

M: How long did you study with Schnabel?

F: Off and on, for ten years in New York, with the interruption of the war. Actually, from 1941 to 1951. He was one very important influence in my studies. I was also influenced by what I read, and by my earlier teachers, one of whom was a lady named Büchenbacher from Fürth, Germany. At age eleven I played for Schnabel at Tremezzo. He said I would eventually study under his tutelage, but then I was too little. He advised that I first study with a pupil of his in Paris who was at the Conservatory there. Their approaches were different. Schnabel did not advise exercises. I once read an article entitled "How do Pianists Practice?" by Gieseking in which he jokingly said; "Once you have practiced your scales, arpeggios, trills, thirds, sixths, and octaves, you know them!" On the other hand, he said in the same article, "It is not enough to know that you are playing unevenly; you have to listen very carefully to know exactly which finger is playing unevenly and correct it." That is one point of view. Serkin spends a great deal of his practice time with scales and exercises. Lately, I have been doing a great many abstract exercises, and am having a great deal of fun with them.

M: What do you mean by abstract exercises?

F: I mean technical studies which are not études or pieces of music having a shape, harmony, and a tune, as in a Chopin *Etude*. I am speaking of exercises which develop and train one aspect of the hand. It is very pleasant to start a day, week, or session after you've been away from the piano for some time, with these exercises—it's like cleaning your equipment. Whenever I can, I spend an hour in this way. I begin first with a Rachmaninoff exercise in double notes. I like to do arpeggios before I do scales. I do them without passing the thumb, going up chromatically. Then, arpeggios all over the keyboard, with and without passing the thumb. Followed by scales, thirds, sixths, octaves, et cetera. This takes approximately an hour. In theory, I would like to do this every time I practice but it isn't always possible. I might add here that there is nobody in the world whose mind doesn't wander when they practice. Very few people admit this, but everybody does it and feels guilty about it. This must happen from time to time. When you practice Mozart, Stravinsky, or Beethoven, it is not very complimentary to think of other things. When you practice exercises, however, it seems perfectly all right to have your mind wander occasionally. For instance, in doing scales, I personally like to do C major, A minor, F major, D minor, and so on through the circle of keys rather than going up chromatically.

M: I find double-note patterns very beneficial. My first teacher insisted upon double thirds and sixths, chromatic thirds, major and minor, when I was ten or eleven. When I came to Josef Lhevinne at the age of fifteen and a half, he asked me to play a scale. I sat down and tossed off double-third scales in contrary motion. He looked at me and asked, "Where did you learn that?" I asked, "Why? Doesn't everybody do it?" When I was young, I used to say to myself when encountering a difficult piece, "Somebody else has played this. I also have ten fingers. Why can't I play it?" Somehow I evolved this philosophy at a very early age.

F: How wonderful to get that under your belt so early in life.

M: This is why I am astonished when a student offers one half-movement of a sonata. We always studied three works at a time with Mr. Lhevinne. Of course at Juilliard, students schedule practice hours around their class commitments. I was one of the original dropouts, for I left school at the age of fifteen. I had one year of high school and am totally self-taught in languages and everything else.

F: When I do these exercises, I feel great. I've noticed that when I've worked at a batch of exercises, I play more relaxedly and can really concentrate on what I want to do interpretively. After all, technique is the ability to do what you want to .

M: It's everything. I played for Walter Gieseking before I went to Berlin to study with Schnabel. He impressed upon me that there is no difference between technique and interpretation. At that time, I really didn't know what music was all about, because I wasn't enough of a musician. My repertoire included many major works when I won the Naumburg Competition. Managers approached me but I knew that my understanding was limited. Mr. Lhevinne, who was phenomenal for pianistic things, sometimes did not delve deeply enough into the music. I wanted still more. I gave up everything in America and went to Berlin to study with Schnabel. I could only afford six lessons with him over a period of two years, but I wouldn't take $100,000 for those lessons now. After my first lesson with him, I came home and my cousin found me at the piano, crying. She said, "Now what are you crying about? You won the Naumburg, you came to Europe, you're studying with a great musician, what's the problem?" I said, "It's as though this man has opened up the Bible of what music is all about for me." She said, "Good—now we can have dinner." From that moment on, I really began to study. I became my own taskmaster, suddenly becoming conscious of everything in music. I recently met Karl Ulrich Schnabel at the Bach International Competition, which we judged together. He told me, "I know that you studied with my father. I want to tell you that there has not been a day in my musical life that I have not thought about what I learned—how he helped me to realize what music is all about, how it's put

62

I can give some students Schoenberg, Webern, Elliott Carter, or something totally avant-garde, and they will bring it completely memorized in one lesson. By contrast, a Mozart sonata in the same length of time will result in one movement barely learned. . .Adele Marcus.

together." Naturally, one has to do a lot on one's own. One must first have a musical concept, the technical equipment to get it out of the piano, and the reasoning or musicianship to understand why we do things.

F: This is a very complex problem, because everyone's approach to the instrument is necessarily different. If you speak to any violin teacher, he or she will tell you that a certain hand or bow position will produce a certain tone, and most of the time, they are right. On the piano, this simply is not so. There is no such thing as a method. A low wrist will not necessarily produce a different tone from a high wrist. It's an entirely individual matter.

M: There is such a thing, however, as a normal position of the hand, attributable to its structure. The four fingers form an even base and move vertically, the thumb is attached to the side and moves laterally. I always say, "Structure is the basis of all movement." If you understand the structure of the hand, you understand how it moves. Personally, I prefer to play more on the cushions of the fingers, rather than with curved fingers.

F: I, on the other hand, play mostly with curved fingers. There are times, of course, when our approaches would overlap.

M: There are so many ways of doing things with the fingers, wrist, and the entire playing mechanism. Whatever we do, however, is motivated by an interpretive sense and by the ear.

F: In piano, the ear must be the final judge. The motion of the hand will follow what the ear dictates.

M: It's a very intimate and individual instrument. For me, the cushion of the finger is the most sensitive and produces the most malleable tone. I play with that part of the finger unless I want something to sound very crisp.

F: Between two people with the same musical ideas, the approach to the instrument and the means of getting the sound out may be entirely different.

M: We cannot arrive at the artist's level until we know many rules and can break them intelligently. When Horowitz was younger, he didn't play the way he does now. He developed a manner of playing with very low wrists because he felt more tonal control this way. He played mainly with the fingers, with very little wrist and arm flexibility. When he was less nervous, he used much more wrist. I'll never forget the time I was sitting in the first row of

Carnegie Hall—his trouser leg shook as though a fan were blowing it, that's how nervous he was. I didn't see how he made it through the first piece.!

F: I simply do not believe in any method. It seems to me that many students nowadays, especially boys, play with rather stiff wrists. Girls seem to have naturally more joint flexibility. I dislike this stiff approach, but if it sounds alright, I don't complain.

M: I have come to the same conclusion in my teaching. If I tell certain students to mold their hand to the pattern of a phrase and to shape it with the wrist, I might as well be speaking a foreign language. I used to think I could make a horse play with a singing tone, but I gave that notion up a long time ago. If some students get a good tone now and then, I'm very grateful. In the final analysis, one makes one's own technique. But when students are beginning, they must be taught a particular approach to the instrument in order to have something concrete. After that, they should break these rules only if need be in order to express something.

F: For example, we know that we both finger-pedal a great deal. However, Mr. Serkin once told me that Busoni pedaled everything in order to play legato, sometimes raising his hands between tones in legato lines, tying it with the pedal.

M: In some music one can do this. I do it in Impressionistic music.

F: But the point is that this approach apparently worked for him in most literature. This is why the ear must ultimately decide.

M: I often show students many ways of playing a passage, demonstrating that I can obtain the same sound with the tip of a pencil, or what have you.

F: This is a point very often discussed amongst pianists. The question is: "Is there such a thing as piano tone, and what makes it?" Hindemith said that it doesn't make any difference what you use to strike the piano—it could be the end of an umbrella.

M: I don't think he really meant that.

F: I think he was basically right. The important thing is who hits it with the end of an umbrella. If a great artist plays one tone with the end of an umbrella, he will play it much more sensitively than if the charwoman does it.

M: I agree. It has been said that if Picasso spit on the sidewalk outside his house, they could frame it and sell it for $500,000, because the way he spit was so different from the way anyone else spit! If anyone else would make a stroke across a canvas, it would just not be the same as if Picasso had done it.

F: On the subject of practicing, I find that people usually admit to less practicing than they actually do. Most people are ashamed of practicing. There is the old saying, "Whoever practices, needs to." There is absolutely nothing wrong with practicing as many hours as it requires to do your best performance. However, one must be aware of dividing one's practice time, and to secure variety in practicing. There must be creative practicing, which you do even if you already know a piece because you want to change your conception or because you have discovered something new in the music. The most mundane type of practicing involves the actual learning of a piece, which is mostly memorizing. The kind of practicing most people are ashamed to admit to is the training kind, in which one practices works which one already knows in order to develop a super-technique. One searches for the security and reliability of being able to play something at any time under any conditions, on any piano, with any kind of distraction. This is an important facet of practicing.

M: How do you usually practice? Let us say when you have your given program for a recital. What do you do just a few days before you play?

F: If it's a program I've played before, I like to do a lot of creative practicing, really making music with the piece, even at the risk of having to change something at the last moment. I practice a great deal for security and to make sure things are technically in order.

M: Do you check memory also, to make sure that you have it securely in your mind?

F: My memory being what it is, I can easily do this away from the piano.

M: Do you think much about your music away from the piano?

F: Yes, very much.

M: When you think about music away from the piano, do you actually have the notes in front of you?

F: No, not usually.

M: When you think about it, you must see something—do you see the notes, the keyboard. . .?

There is one exception to my otherwise rather rigorous rule about not isolating difficult passages first: when the technical problems are not nervous problems. . .but are purely muscular, physical things like a trill, or an octave passage. . .Claude Frank.

If you speak to any violin teacher, he or she will tell you that a certain hand or bow position will produce a certain tone, and most of the time, they are right. On the piano, this is simply not so. . .A low wrist will not necessarily produce a different tone from a high wrist. . .Claude Frank.

F: No, I see nothing. I can sing it inside, and hear it with the inner ear.

M: This is very interesting. I always see the music, and visualize the score when I do this. What do you do on the occasion of an important concert or recital in one of the big musical centers if you have not played there for a long time? What is your routine on the day of your performance? Do you practice a lot that day, or don't you practice at all?

F: What I like to do best (and this is not always attainable) is to go to the hall around 10 A.M. and practice a good four hours on the piano I am to play. I really get used to the piano, the hall, the program. If I like it, I may continue until around two o'clock. Then I eat a big lunch and rest. If I'm lucky, I return to the hall early. If there is a piano backstage, I practice exercises—no more passages just before the concert.

M: That's pretty much what I like to do.

F: Of course, this does not always happen. There may not be a piano backstage, or there's another rehearsal going on, or they're hammering away at something in the hall, fixing the seats, any number of distractions. In these cases, I prefer to return to the hall as late as possible.

M: When I was playing a great deal, I found that I liked to go to the hall for two short periods. The first time, the piano sometimes felt strange. The second time, it felt different and comfortable. I advise my students, if possible, to arrive a day earlier and work on the piano, then go home and sleep, returning to get the whole ambiance of that particular auditorium. I have found this very helpful, although it's almost never possible. Mr. Horowitz has told me that he likes to go to the hall many, many times and play in order to feel that this is his own piano stool, et cetera. These are, of course, ideal circumstances. We must train ourselves, however, not to expect such conditions every time.

F: I don't believe in spoiling myself to that extent. I would never travel with my own instrument even if I could afford it. I feel it is part of the pianist's responsibility to be as independent of his surroundings as possible. I enjoy the surprise of a more brilliant piano, or a more beautiful piano, or a harder piano.

M: You seem to be the ideal traveling artist who adjusts to all circumstances, difficult as they may be.

"His Liszt playing is without peer in the world today."
—HAROLD C. SCHONBERG, NEW YORK TIMES

Columbia Artists presents

Jorge BOLET

"One of the few living superpianists." —ALAN KRIEGSMAN, WASHINGTON POST

CARNEGIE HALL

Tuesday, May 3rd at 8:00 p.m.

All LISZT PROGRAM: Six Consolations, Sonata in B Minor,
3 Sonatas from Annees de Pelerinage, Book II, Don Juan Fantaisie

Tickets:: $5.50, $4.50, $3.50, $3.00, $2.50 at Box Office
or Call Chargit: 489-9320. Students and Senior Citizens ½ price with ID

JORGE BOLET

Bolet began his piano studies in his native Cuba at the age of five and became a student of David Saperton's at the Curtis Institute when he was twelve. Acknowledged today as one of the world's great musical artists, Mr. Bolet has toured steadily and performed with the world's major orchestras and conductors.

His musical background, romantic temperament, and special affinity for the works of Liszt have made him particularly welcome on the contemporary concert platform where he has been hailed as a genuine musical descendant of Godowsky, Hofmann, and Horowitz.

Marcus: It is a genuine pleasure to be able to discuss the many aspects of your great artistry, remarkable technique, and keyboard approach to study and practice with you personally. How did you begin?

Bolet: When I was very young, probably the most important indication of what was to come was the fact that I had an extremely natural facility for anything mechanical at the keyboard. Because I was an extremely fast learner, I never felt the need, fortunately, to practice endless hours. Somehow I felt that I could learn in one hour what some of my classmates took four hours to accomplish. *Facility* was the prime factor.

Secondly, I started studying with my sister when I was six and a half or seven years old. She was a very talented young lady who must have really taught me extremely well, because after studying with her for five years, I was admitted to the Curtis Institute. There my teacher didn't have to correct any purely mechanical aspects of my technique. He more or less took off from where I was. Apparently, at the age of twelve, I was very much on the right road. I think it is very important for the younger generation to have the correct kind of training right from the very first day.

M: I'm very pleased to hear you say that because, so often, parents will say, "It doesn't matter to whom I send my child first, does it?" I disagree with that point of view!

What do you feel brought you into the closest contact with the instrument when you wanted to really express something? And when you began to experiment with the instrument, how did you proceed?

B: I don't believe in any school of piano-playing. I believe that you have to play whatever you're playing in such a manner as to achieve the result you want in sound, texture, and color. The individuality of the instrument also plays a big part. I heard a rather amusing anecdote not so long ago. A friend of mine was talking to an acquaintance and asked her, "Are you going to Bolet's recital tomorrow?" "No," she answered, "I'm not." My friend inquired, "Why not? You know, he's really a wonderful artist." The reply came: "But I've been told that he places his hands on the keyboard in such a strange position." This is absurd, because nobody plays with more curved fingers than I do. However, at times, I literally play with completely flat fingers; it gives one an entirely different kind of sound. You remember Hofmann and the way he handled a melodic line, with a completely relaxed hand, as though there were no bones in it? This helped him to achieve that soft, ethereal, lyrical sound.

M: I'm sure only those who perform at a high level of professional excellence understand that playing on the cushion of the finger produces the most caressing tone. That's where touch sensitivity lies in the finger. Also, one can press the key down more deeply. There's no rigid hand position.

Have you ever felt the need for a technical routine—stretching exercises, exclusive of etudes?

When I was very young, probably the most important indication of what was to come was the fact that I had an extremely natural facility for anything mechanical at the keyboard. Because I was an extremely fast learner, I never felt the need, fortunately, to practice endless hours. . Jorge Bolet.

B: When I was a little boy, I remember that my sister used to stretch my hand. Particularly the spaces between the fingers. She would flatten the palm of the hand so as to stretch the hand from one end to the other.

M: But you, yourself, did not really practice any stretching exercises?

B: No, not particularly, but Mr. Saperton suggested my working on a good number of exercises, mostly from the Joseffy *School of Advanced Piano-Playing*. I use these studies very religiously with my students.

M: When you worked on a more advanced level, how did you go about experimenting with different textures of sound? Did you employ the pedal very much? Was the wrist and/or arm an aid to your keyboard approach? Can you put into words some of the things you experienced during your experimentation?

B: I think varieties of touch and texture, as we like to call them, are achieved with a combination of the hand and fingers, in addition to the discriminate use of the pedal. I find, in listening to young performers and to my own students, that they have a tendency to over-pedal everything. They use tremendous quantities of pedal.

M: Or none at all!

B: I wish they would use no pedal more often. When I'm playing a running passage, for example, I try to remember that there is really no such thing as a passage in music. To me, all of music is singing; everything must sing. I like to think of passages, let's say, of sixteenth-notes in a Mozart concerto or sonata, as a fast melodic line. They must be shaped and played exactly as though they belonged to a melodic line, with the correct nuance, ascending and descending. If I want a passage to sound like a string of perfectly well-matched pearls, I play with very, very close fingers. One might almost imagine the keyboard smeared with glue; the fingers literally stick to the keys, one after the other. By the same token, if I want a very crisp, dry sound, I play with high fingers, but not necessarily detached. This will automatically produce an entirely different texture.

M: The wide range of dynamics and color in your playing also shows how deftly you use the pedal. I think the pedal serves the piano as a vibrato does the violin. Pedaling is such a great study and art.

B: It certainly is. We have two pedals with which to work: the *damper* pedal, sometimes called the *loud* pedal (I don't really care for the word *loud*), and the *shift*, or *soft*, pedal. In the process of lifting the dampers off the strings, and in the short space of travel between using no pedal and complete pedal, there are literally twenty or thirty different degrees of pressure one can use. The more you lift the dampers, the freer the strings are to vibrate. Many times I use a quarter-pedal, eighth-pedal, and so on. Sometimes I look into the piano because, on some pianos, especially the Baldwin, one can see the actual position of the dampers on the strings. I purposely lift the damper pedal just enough so that it doesn't completely dampen the tone, leaving just the tiniest bit of vibration to the string. This applies to the shift pedal as well; one can press it all the way down, halfway, a quarter, an eighth and so on.

M: I'm so happy to hear you discuss this, because I feel that not enough attention is given to the study of the pedal. This applies to students and some young artists who are already embarking upon careers. The experimentation is endless for the foot must be as sensitive as the fingers; and pedaling is a very great art.

B: Absolutely!

M: Relating to that, I am so annoyed at today's shoe styles, especially those with very thick soles. It has become a major factor in my teaching to insist that students bring two pairs of shoes to their lessons: the ones they walk in, and a pair with thin soles for playing the piano. They don't realize how important it is to feel how far down the pedal is going, how important it is to make a crescendo or diminuendo with the *loud* pedal, as you say. There are so many ways of making inverted pedalings. This must not become a separate study, but completely indigenous to the entire learning experience.

B: Definitely. One place where young pianists invariably pedal poorly is in *fortissimo* chord playing which requires absolute clarity. When a chord is played, a tremendous amount of resonance comes from the instrument. Then, to play another chord immediately afterwards requires split-second release of the pedal to clarify the changing harmony. I'm very sensitive to this "overhang" from the previous harmony. This, to me, is always very upsetting.

M: Clarity certainly takes a very special coordination of foot, hands, and ear, in addition to keyboard approach, don't you think?

B: Yes, but I think it's mainly a question of releasing the pedal long enough to dampen the previous sonority before you put it down again for the sonority that you've just played.

M: Could you tell me how you feel about sitting close or far from the piano, high or low?

B: I think one must always sit in such a way that the elbow is far enough away from the torso so that one can get the elbow into one's torso. If one sits too close to the keyboard, as many students do, the elbow is right at the side of the torso and inhibits the inward movement of the elbow.

M: I realize, too, that it depends upon the height of a person whether one sits further away or closer.

B: It also depends upon the girth of a person! (Fortunately, I don't have any really fat students!) As to the height, I believe one should sit as low as one possibly can, comfortably.

M: Why?

B: When one sits at the keyboard, the line from the elbow to the hands should make, basically, a horizontal line, or perhaps the elbow could be a bit lower than the hand at the keyboard. If the elbow is higher, the tendency is to produce a harsher, more brittle sound.

One place where young pianists invariably pedal poorly is in fortissimo chord-playing which requires absolute clarity. When a chord is played, a tremendous amount of resonance comes from the instrument. Then, to play another chord immediately afterwards requires split-second release of the pedal to clarify the changing harmony. . Jorge Bolet.

77

M: It's a very difficult subject. I suppose we can't designate to anyone exactly how high or low, or how close or how far back from the instrument one should sit. It depends largely upon the stature and upon the feeling of the hand. I agree with you, however, that sitting a little too low is better than too high. Yet there are many small hands which have more span over the keyboard when sitting a little higher. The hand stretches out more easily than when reaching up to the keyboard.

B: It is, of course, an individual problem.

M: You once mentioned to me something about dotted rhythmic patterns for study; I don't think you believe in this practice, and I don't either.

B: No, I don't believe in it! Many of my students ask if they should practice difficult passages in varying rhythmic patterns. As far as I'm concerned, it's a total waste of time. What I have said about accentuation is that I practice scales in groups of four. I start out by playing the first note of the group as *fortissimo* as I can, not using an arm accentuation, but trying to play from the top knuckle of the finger down. In other words, I play as strong an accent as I can without helping myself with the hand, wrist, or arm.

M: And you believe in practicing this way very close to the keys?

B: Yes, very close to the keys, with the finger on the surface of the key, giving it a very strong push downward. Think of that as a *fortissimo* accent, let's say. Then I play the next three notes in the group as *pianissimo* as I can, but they must all be exactly even; one must not be louder than any of the others. Then the next group in exactly the same way, up four octaves, down four octaves. Then I start again, accenting the second note of each group with all others *pianissimo*; then the third, and so on.

M: Do you suggest doing this with both hands together, or separately?

B: I find that if the student is not able to coordinate the two hands at the beginning, he should practice hands separately.

M: I've never heard of this procedure before, and I find it exceedingly interesting. When you have a beautiful melodic phrase, do you shape your wrist to the pattern of the phrase, or do you play much more from the hands and fingers? Naturally, one cannot say that every phrase is the same, for that would be comparable to saying that every sentence is the same. But in general, are you conscious of a wrist movement which, by opening the hand, embraces the whole pattern?

B: No, I don't believe very much in this "rolling" kind of motion.

M: But I don't mean rolling—rather molding.

B: No, not really. A couple of years ago Indiana University videotaped an entire recital of mine which was put on Public Broadcasting System shortly afterwards. When I saw the playback, I was really amazed at the great variety of motions I went through in playing many things, of which I really was not aware.

M: I think it's always amazing how many things we do quite naturally, and very successfully. I find that those who are achieving a variety of sound and are making the sound as malleable as possible—perhaps not as malleable as yours in color and tonal variety—have to use the wrist, even if they're not conscious of it.

B: It isn't that I do not use the wrist, but I don't consciously make an effort to use it. Producing the kind of sound that I want has become so automatic that I really don't know how I do it.

M: That's excellent; I know exactly what you mean. If a passage in music dictates something to you at sight, you can do it without having to work for it. You may search for certain proportions, but many details emerge the first time as well as at any other time, and sometimes better.

B: That's true, especially if one has an instrument which responds perfectly to every nuance. Many times, for the particular shaping of a phrase or in making a negative accent, for example, I absolutely must try it out on a particular instrument. Otherwise, the very voicing of the piano may destroy the desired effect.

M: I understand. Jorge, tell me how you approach melodic works interpretively.

B: In the melodic playing of a Chopin nocturne, for example, I sometimes have to battle with certain students. Each one of my students must always play a simple, poetic, lyrical work. I might give him a Beethoven Sonata or some other large-scale work, but a Schumann *Romanza*, the Intermezzo from the *Faschingsschwank aus Wien*, a Chopin nocturne, or something of that order must be in the process of preparation. In a piece of that kind, I believe in studying every phrase and analyzing every harmonic progression. It is important to formulate clearly what I call *points of arrival*.

Every phrase dictates its own shape. The harmonic structure also shows the proper direction.

M: So few people seem to feel the breadth and depth of a great melodic line and allow it to sing out, without too much intrusion from the left hand. The bass is important, we know, but should not overshadow the melody.

B: I would put it a little differently. I like to tell my students that, in all the recorded history of music performance, no one has ever paid admission into a concert hall to hear an Alberti Bass.

M: Excellent—I love that! What do you suggest further in viewing students, not only in their study, but in their performing careers?

B: As you know, I hear a great many young people play in competitions and recitals, including my own students. I find that most of their difficulties revolve around the fact that they don't train themselves to listen to what they're doing. I think it's the fact that they're so involved with the complexities of what they're trying to do that they think *before* they play, but they don't hear *after* they play. Whatever we do must always be the result of what we've already heard. We must constantly make an infinite number of adjustments as we play. Their balances of left hand and right hand are often very, very poor, in my opinion.

M: Then, of course, when we look at the other end of the spectrum, I think it was Hofmann who said, "By their left hands, ye shall know them." But this has a different connotation. It means, I think, that if the left hand is superficial and doesn't have real articulation and sonority when it has important passages, the endurance, clarity, lightness, and speed are sacrificed. Don't you believe that?

B: We must certainly be able to do anything with the left hand that we can with the right hand. Tonal balance is an area which all young pianists must become aware of and study carefully.

M: What about literature for developing the student toward a career?

B: I think a young pianist really should play as vast a repertoire as possible. It is very important to play all styles of music. Anyone who intends to become a major figure in the pianistic world must, by the age of twenty, have the technical equipment to play anything ever written for the piano. From the age of twenty to

80

thirty, I believe he should play as wide a variety of music as possible: contemporary, baroque, classical, romantic, everything—primarily to find out the kinds of music with which he personally identifies. Even within one period, there are compositions which suit us particularly and those which do not. From thirty on, it's merely a question of going on, studying, playing, gaining experience, and becoming more personally involved with one's own approach to music.

M: Don't you feel that it's very important to examine periodically where one has come from and where one is going, much in the way a large department store takes inventory? We are never at the same point of development; we are always searching for something more, better, deeper. Would you suggest that young people seek advice from teachers, or do you advise that they go off by themselves and work alone, so that they can find their own identity in music? I realize this is an individual thing, but don't you think too many strong opinions from others can also be distracting in establishing one's own individuality?

B: I think, as I said before, that it is very important to have the very best training right from the beginning. Naturally, there comes a time when the teacher who first taught you the C-major scale is not able to teach you many other things, and you must go to someone else. However, I feel that teacher-hopping never does any good. These students who study with one teacher for six months to get an idea on one piece are accomplishing absolutely nothing. It is very important to stay with a teacher long enough to absorb fully and assimilate everything that teacher has to offer.

M: I agree with you. I feel that you have to be able to judge your own weaknesses and strengths. It is comparable to saying, "This is me." One of the most difficult points in the teacher-pupil relationship is to establish this realistic appraisal, this constructive objectivity.

B: Yes, it is! In accepting a new student, I often find the first year or two rather experimental in that the student hasn't either accepted or understood what our objectives are. However, by the end of the second year, the responses are solid, principles have been applied, and progress is obvious. This is why, when many people come to me and say, "I am playing a recital in Tully Hall in three months and would like to play my program for your advice," I say,

"I'm terribly sorry, but you can't do things that way. Whatever I will tell you might confuse you so that my opinions might do more harm than good," and I just flatly turn them down.

M: I very often do the same thing, especially if I feel that the person is not even ready for a New York recital! How do you evaluate a young competition candidate—one who is seeking scholarship aid, and one who wishes to embark immediately upon a career?

B: If it's a question of scholarships for further study, I believe in giving the prize to the contestant who shows the greatest potential and natural gift; both pianistically and musically. He might not be as advanced in mechanical matters or even as a musician as yet, but he may have a certain spark which shows the capacity to grow. As far as the big international competitions which supposedly launch careers, I find that the contestant who can play everything equally well generally comes out on top. However, there seem to be too many people who play everything well, but who may never be able to play anything superbly.

M: I agree with you. Of course, we cannot always predict the ultimate development.

B: I look for somebody who can keep my interest in what he is playing whether I agree with his approach or not. At least, one who shows a personal insight into music-making which keeps me on the edge of my seat, as it were.

M: In other words, you feel that the personality has to be able to project itself through the composer's music. We are all trying to

I think varieties of touch and texture, as we like to call them, are achieved with a combination of the hand and the fingers, in addition to the discriminate use of the pedal. I find, in listening to young performers and to my own students, that they have a tendency to over-pedal everything. . Jorge Bolet.

express what the composer means, but the performer's individuality also has to communicate in a convincing way. Is this what you mean?

B: You know me well enough, Adele, to know that if I am anything in this world, I am not a purist when it comes to music. I feel very strongly that, if music is the art of communication between two human beings by means of musical sound, there's nothing deader than a written piece of music. To me, this is absolutely nothing. It is just the product of a great musical mind, a genius, who had this idea and was able to put it down in certain conventional black and white symbols which we call a musical score. However, I think that the writing down of a piece of music accounts for fifty per-cent of a performance. The other fifty percent is what the performer is able to read into that piece of music and how he can interpret it. It must be, after all, an interpretation of what the composer wrote.

M: You feel, in other words, that piano-playing is a "creatively re-creative" art, and must also be creative on the part of the interpreter. Otherwise, all of the great scores would have remained on the shelf if important artistic re-creators had not interpreted them.

B: I'm glad that you use the words creative and creator. I feel that the other half of a composer's creation belongs necessarily to the performer.

M: I think that's an excellent way to put it. Fortunately, I do believe, in this era we are leading more toward the freedom of what the person feels, thinks, and has been able to crystallize *through* the eyes of the composer, with the aid of their guidelines. On the other hand, we have the other side of the spectrum, the purists who say, *"Piano* is *piano,* and *forte* is *forte."* As you said before, of course, there's no absolute *forte, piano* or any other marking. It's very difficult to get this across to most students; they then think one can-

We have two pedals with which to work: the damper pedal, sometimes called the loud pedal, and the shift, or soft pedal. In the process of lifting the dampers of the strings, and in the short space of travel between using no pedal and complete pedal, there are literally twenty or thirty different degrees of pressure one can use. . .Jorge Bolet.

Dr. Trübenbach - Berlin 1975

A4478

not possibly be a musician. What do you feel a musician is, anyway?

B: I believe a musician is a person who, first of all, has an open mind about everything in connection with music. He is a person who is willing to listen to anything, regardless of how absurd it might appear on the surface; a person who is willing to study and consider all angles and approaches to music, open to all ideas, and sufficiently learned to make a choice as to what he wants to do and the road that he wants to follow.

M: Bravo! In other words, he is a reasoning person.

B: He must be someone who is honest enough to realize that his way is not the only way, but that it is the only way in which he personally can proceed.

M: I'm so happy to hear you say that. Very often, I might suggest my own interpretive convictions to a student who has played only a blueprint of the score. I will give him ideas, and then I say, "This may not be the only way but, if you have a real concept of your own, it must be convincing from a musician's standpoint, all the way through." It must not be fragments of Rubinstein, Rachmaninoff, Horowitz, or Serkin. You have to go to the source, which is the music, to find the roots of your interpretation, and then assimilate it in your own way, if you have sufficient authority.

B: That's right; it's a personal way of understanding the music you play. Many times we restudy a piece which we haven't played in many years and, in the course of those years, so much has happened—we have learned so much, perhaps have deepened our emotional lives or our attitudes toward a lot of things—and we're able to see many, many things in that score of which we were not aware before.

M: I love that great saying of Godowsky: "In your youth, you play with all your virtuosity and flair; in middle age, you show what a deep musician you are; and, as you get older, you look for the inner voices." However, I feel that looking for the inner voices has not only to do with contrapuntal awareness; I think it has also to do with the inner voices which say things to us as more mature people, don't you think so?

B: Yes. Different emphases, which give different shades of meaning and importance, are all part of an artist's craft and interpretive concepts.

86

RUDOLF FIRKUSNY

Rudolf Firkusny was born in Napajedlá, Czechoslovakia. At the age of four, he began picking out tunes on the piano, but did not make his debut until he was ten, when he performed a Mozart concerto with the Prague Philharmonic in the capital. Firkusny has concertized extensively in Europe and America. His repertoire is extraordinarily varied. Today, he divides his time between touring, recording, and teaching at the Juilliard School where he has been on the faculty since 1965.

Marcus: Looking back over your long and illustrious career, what do you now feel was the most significant influence in leading you, ultimately, to achieve such a high artistic level?

Firkusny: I began my studies as a very small child under the guidance of the great Czech composer Leos Janácek. Janácek did not intend for me to become "just a pianist." He did not want to teach me to play the piano; he wished to supervise my general musical education, since I was already composing to some extent. He did find a piano teacher for me, but his idea was to educate me as a musician first. In the beginning, my piano-playing, per se, was always the expression of *my* musical ideas, or those of the composers I studied, not the outcome of systematic study of the piano. That I developed as a pianist was a result of much practicing throughout many years.

M: How old were you when you began?

F: I came to the piano when I was not quite four, but I met Janácek when I was five.

M: You had that strong an influence exerted upon you at the age of five!

F: Yes, I was with him for a number of years. He was primarily a guide and a musical mentor. Of course, I went to school and had to do everything else besides. Music was always comparable to a hobby. I was never forced to practice; Janácek had a horror of child

87

prodigies. I did appear publicly, however. At my debut I was actually a child. My piano teachers were not as opposed to my public exhibition as Janacek was, but they didn't encourage it. I think this is quite important.

M: With whom did you study piano?

F: My first teacher was a man who was not actually a pianist; he was a flute-player. He accepted me when I was about three and a half or four years old.

M: Did you have a perfect pitch?

F: Yes, always. I didn't know it at that time, but later Janácek found out by giving me an examination. I learned how to read music with this first teacher, but I didn't learn anything about actual piano-playing. After a short time, I decided I didn't want to stay with him; I said, "I know everything I need to know", and I just played. I played whatever came to my mind; I had a very good memory.

M: Did you read music?

F: Yes, in my own way, of course.

M: You did not learn by rote?

F: No.

M: You were able to read the treble and bass clefs.

F: Yes. However, my greatest pleasure was just to play. I improvised a lot. When I heard something at a concert in Prague, I came home and played it. Then, somehow, Janácek heard about this curious child. He had a very bad reputation as a rather unpleasant and difficult man. When he wanted to hear me, many of my mother's friends discouraged her, saying, "Don't bring your child to that maniac!" But I wanted to go. I played the *Eighth Slavonic Dance* by Dvorák and a small piece which was a folk tune from an opera by Janácek. He then gave me several examinations and told my mother that I was remarkably talented. Janácek of-

I have learned to stay away from too much sight-reading; it's a bit dangerous. In other words, it was easy for me to learn an entire piece. However, what came easily in the music I would never practice—only what was difficult. Therefore, I could learn a piece superficially very quickly, but not in depth. . .Rudolf Firkusny.

fered to take care of my general musical education, starting with composition. The piano teacher he found for me was a fine lady pianist and harpist. This was the beginning of my first serious piano study. Soon thereafter she took a leave of absence and I was brought to a new teacher, Vilem Kurz. His great reputation preceded him. Until the time he arrived in Czechoslovakia, he had been teaching in L'vov (at that time part of Austria, later Poland, and now Russia). His daughter was an excellent pianist. Great fame came eventually to this wonderful pedagogue.

M: Were your parents musical?

F: No.

M: You were the only really big talent in the family?

F: Yes. I started to play, as a matter of fact, shortly after my father died when I was three years old. My mother, with three small children to care for during the first year of World War I, was in pretty bad shape. We had a piano in the house, but she decided that nobody should play.

M: Your musical education really stemmed, then, from a total love of music, not the instrument, essentially.

F: Yes. I told Janácek that I would love to go to Kurz. He suggested that I work with Mme. Kurz first because, for a child, a woman teacher is better than a man, possibly a little more understanding.

M: How did you begin? Were you given some kind of technical exercises?

F: Yes. Kurz had a very, very strict regime. By the way, Steuermann was also his pupil . He used a combination method which was successful for him. He considered the fingers very important and advised having a completely loose, free arm so that one could play for a considerable length of time without feeling tired or exhausted.

M: You had to go through a regimen.

F: Yes. That was for everyone, advanced students as well as beginners. We were given exercises exclusively for one month. These exercises were comprised of five-note patterns and scales. Everything had to be done very, very slowly and with great concentration. If we made a little mistake he went into fits. His wife was very gentle. She was, however, afraid of him because he always supervised the lessons. Simple preludes by Bach, small Mozart

90

pieces, and little Czech sonatinas were then added. Etudes came later; he didn't want me to start études right away. The only études he considered good were the small Czerny studies.

M: Do you feel that Chopin *Etudes* are masterpieces and should not be used merely as technical exercises?

F: I don't see anything wrong with using them as exercises. Of course, there's a great difference between playing them as études and playing them as masterpieces. You have to have a certain physical dexterity to be able to overcome the technical problems and give something more. As a young student, I didn't even touch Chopin because I couldn't reach an octave; we were limited to the things which required very little span, because my teacher didn't want to force my hand; he wanted a normal development.

M: What age were you then?

F: I was seven. Then we started learning the Mozart Concerto, which I played with orchestra for the first time. Of course, we began to study études by Cramer, Clementi and Czerny, later.

M: But you were compelled to go through that whole thing. At what time did you reach a higher kind of development?

F: I finished at the Conservatory with Kurz's wife. I was in her class but Mr. Kurz was always around. In Czechoslovakia we had what was called *Meisterklass*. We had to finish the Conservatory first and then were placed automatically in Mr. Kurz's master class. Even then, he would come back to the exercises a little, not for long, but for periods of time we would forget everything and concentrate on them. Under Kurz, I finished the *Meisterklass* with a diploma, and then, inevitably, I began to have different ideas about many things. He was a wonderful teacher, but he was very strict—a bit of a slave-driver.

M: Did you have chamber music in your studies?

F: That I did at home—I played not only chamber music, but every score I could lay my hands on: operas, symphonies, four hands or alone, you name it. As I said, the piano was always a kind of hobby; I practiced, but not terribly hard. When I started to concertize, I always did improvisations; the audience supplied the themes.

M: Do you still improvise?

F: I stopped when I started to study composition seriously. When I was a child I didn't know whether I would be a composer, conductor, or pianist. I happened to become a pianist. But I always wanted to be an all-around musician, to be able to do anything.

M: I can well understand that.

F: I love the piano, but I was never in love with it to such a degree that nothing else existed. It was a wonderful way of expressing yourself, because the piano is the most complete instrument aside from the orchestra.

M: Have you ever played another instrument?

F: No. I started to play the violin, but was unsuccessful, and Janacek told me not to continue.

M: How old were you when you began to compose?

F: When I was about six years old. At seven I played my own composition, which was called *Humoreske*. It is very similar to Dvorak's; mine is in F-sharp major, his is in G-flat major! Everybody asked me if it were my father's or my uncle's and Janacek smiled and said it was my own. I composed many small pieces all the time. I also wrote a cadenza for the *Coronation Concerto* which I finally didn't use because it was rather strange.

Janáček's teaching was absolutely unorthodox. We would sometimes spend entire lessons playing *Pelléas et Mélisande* or *Petrouchka*, which at that time were completely new for us. He played his compositions for me and vice versa. It was giving me an idea of what music is, what it represents, its enormous scope.

M: Have you written any vocal music?

F: Yes, I wrote many songs.

M: In writing, did you favor the voice, orchestra, chamber music, or piano?

F: Actually, my least successful works were for piano. I wrote a piano concerto with which I finished my *Meisterklass* in Prague, and performed it only once. It was horrible writing for the piano; Kurz just couldn't believe that a pianist could write so badly for his own instrument!

M: That is fascinating!

F: Janácek urged me to begin the serious study of composition. I entered the Conservatory as a composer and finished as a pianist. My studies began with harmony and counterpoint, and I gave up improvising publicly.

M: Did you study piano with anyone other than Mr. Kurz?

F: No. When our work together had finished, I had a tremendous need to become myself. He was, in this case, a little strange; he was so jealous of everything, and very possessive. He started to close in on me, which I couldn't take. So I broke loose. I was fortunate that the man who helped me financially in my studies was the President of Czechoslovakia, Thomas Masaryk. Because we had a difficult situation at home, he assisted me through my formal schooling at the Gymnasium.

M: Did you enjoy it?

F: Not very much, but I did it. President Masaryk, as compensation for finishing all my studies, allowed me to leave Czechoslovakia for one year, so I went to Paris. I wanted to study with Cortot, but I did not work with him privately. I merely went to many classes, listened a lot, and attended all the concerts I possibly could. Cortot refused to teach me; I played for him and he told me that I didn't need a teacher, but a public. He engaged me to play in a concert which he conducted in Paris.

M: How old were you then?

F: About nineteen.

M: Whatever you achieved musically as a young student apparently stood you in good stead later on. Approximately how many hours a day did you work at the piano?

F: I couldn't work very much because I was in school all day and when I came home, I had just a few hours left; I doubt that I practiced more than two or three hours maximum.

M: What music did you lean toward the most?

F: Opera; it was my joy. When I wanted to have a great time for myself, I went through the scores of Verdi and Wagner.

M: Of course, you've always been a good sight-reader and you have a very retentive memory. When you emerged as a pianist accepting engagements, how did you work, how did you study?

F: The great difference in the way we study as adults, it seems to me, is that while the approach is more or less the same, we explore more musical possibilities in depth. Then, of course, we have to work on the technical difficulties as well. Naturally, I could not always be at a piano, so my great joy was to take the music to bed with me. I tried to understand its content and to establish an eventual concept of it. Then I would go to the piano. As I said before, when I was young I was a very good sight-reader. I think this is a great disadvantage.

M: Why?

F: I have learned to stay away from too much sight-reading; it's a bit dangerous. In other words, it was easy for me to learn an entire piece. However, what came easily in the music I would never practice—only what was difficult. Therefore, I could learn a piece superficially very quickly, but not in depth.

M: Could you immediately formulate, by singing melodic passages and thematic material, the exact way you would like to phrase a piece or did you always go to the piano for that?

F: You have to go the piano for that phrasing, because music is a language of sound. Sometimes it's a question of purely physical possibilities; sometimes you have to use a certain fingering that's more comfortable for your hand than the one which musically may be more correct. These things you have to do at the piano.

M: How did you get from the initial stages of your study, such as studying the music away from the piano, playing it, and making your own decisions, to the point at which you were totally familiar with a composition? How does the procedure differ? Also, how do you prepare for a concert?

F: If you already know a work, and have played it, then the *real* work must start, because you realize everything you didn't do before which you want to do later. I must say that every time I play something, it's like I'm playing it for the first time. I take it very seriously; I don't take anything for granted. I look back at the score, I go back to the notes. I use the music while practicing; I don't trust my memory. Of course, I discover some things which I didn't recognize before.

Taken in 1971 at the Juilliard Concert Hall, this photograph features the Juilliard Quartet with Rudolf Firkusny. Left to right: Robert Mann (violin), Claus Adam (cello), Firkusny, Samuel Rhodes (viola) and Earl Carlyss (violin).

95

M: And you question all editions, do you not?

F: All kinds; whatever I can put my hands on.

M: And also, when you make a decision, let us say, and you try different fingerings for expressiveness, not only for comfort and vice versa, do you practice right hand alone, left hand alone? Do you take long sections, or do you generally take very small sections?

F: Sometimes I practice hands separately in contrapuntal works or in very complicated music, but when it's not absolutely necessary, I would rather use both hands. Of course, I practice slowly. Very slowly.

M: Do you feel that it's very important, even when something is still rough, to play it through in order to get the feeling of the piece in its entirety; then go back to see where it's not up to the standard that you want?

F: Yes, it definitely helps. When I was young I was much more adventurous and didn't take my work as seriously as I do now. I played, and somehow it was all right. So I said, "Its ready. Now, it takes me much longer, and I work very hard before I feel that it is ready! Sometimes I am asked, "Can you do it?" and I say, "One can do anything, but I can't promise that even the simplest piece will be learned in one or two weeks." It could take me a day or perhaps a year; I don't know. It's becoming worse and worse every year of my adult life.

M: It's amazing how terribly hard we have to work to meet our own escalating standards. We begin to demand the ultimate. Young students, naturally, do not always appreciate this.

F: I have to work very hard. It was very easy when I was very small. When you realize how truly difficult it is, then the hard times come. I went to Schnabel later at Lake Como in Italy for advice. But the hard work really began when I was on my own. As long as I had a teacher, someone was exercising control over me, and would tell me exactly what was wrong and what was right. When you are on your own, then you really become your most severe critic.

M: Have you had the experience of working on a composition and developing a very definite concept, then putting it away? Later, when you come back to it, you find that you are quite another person?

F: Absolutely.

M: It is not always that you want to change an interpretation, but rather that *you* have changed, and your reactions are completely different. When you have arrived at that point, and I'm sure you have many times, what was your procedure: starting from scratch, or trying to recapture what you did before?

F: No, many times I have wanted to start from scratch, to forget everything else. But those things which were child's play when I was fourteen or fifteen suddenly became frightfully challenging.

M: Now that you are a great and established artist, which composers would you say helped you to grow the most?

F: That's easy to say: Mozart, number one; Chopin, number two; and Debussy, number three.

M: Why?

F: I think these are the three composers who wrote the most ideally for the piano. I'm not speaking of music in general; just for the pianist. Of course, I love—I adore—Schumann, but he is much more intellectual. It's a different thing. But for piano-playing I think these three composers are somehow always the greatest test.

M: Because their music is so transparent that it is immediately obvious whether you can or can't play them. There's nothing to hide behind.

F: When I was a child I didn't like Mozart because I played it too much. I didn't like it at all. Mozart is too often given to children, which is very wrong. I wanted to play Liszt and Tchaikovsky—big, flashy things. But my teacher said, "No, we have to go slowly." Then, I completely abandoned Mozart for quite a while. Finally, I went to Schnabel and studied some Mozart with him. Suddenly, I began to discover how much I loved Mozart, but also realized how terribly difficult his music is.

I remember very well when Erich Kleiber asked me to play the Mozart D Minor Concerto, K. 466, with him. I hadn't played it since my childhood. I was terribly nervous, and I went to the rehearsal and told Kleiber, "I can't tell you how nervous I am." He said, "Don't worry, I am too." Then I started to really understand Mozart, and I began to love him even more. His music is very vocal, yes, but also so brilliant in many ways. My affinity for Schubert came rather later.

A 1338

M: Schubert is a very challenging composer. Which do you think is more challenging now: Schubert or Mozart?

F: They're very different. Mozart is always challenging because it's so simple, in a way. And yet it's not simple, at the same time. Schubert, of course, is difficult from another point of view: the emotion, the length. But somehow, everything is there, in a certain sense.

M: To recapture, the "Innigkeit" (inner feeling) constantly is so demanding.

F: It is, for example, easier to play the opening of Schubert's B-flat-major *Sonata* than to play the B-flat-major *Romanza* of Mozart's D-minor *Concerto*, although the "Innigkeit" is the same. To invest a work with genuine feeling without bad taste or over-sentimentalization is difficult.

M: Do you think Beethoven is as demanding as Mozart and Schubert?

F: Beethoven is somewhat easier than both, in a sense. It is invariably more difficult pianistically, and the music itself is usually more complex. But it reaches us more directly. The character and mood can be more easily projected.

M: When you play a work of Beethoven, and formulate a very satisfying concept of it—be it sonata, concerto, or chamber music—doesn't it tend to remain firmly grounded?

F: Yes, it seems more definite.

When I was a child I didn't like Mozart because I played it too much. I didn't like it at all. Mozart is too often given to children, which is very wrong. I wanted to play Liszt and Tchaikovsky—big, flashy things. But my teacher said, "No, we have to go slowly." Then, I completely abandoned Mozart for quite a while. Finally, I went to Schnabel and studied some Mozart with him. Suddenly, I began to discover how much I loved Mozart, but also realized how terribly difficult his music is.. . .Rudolf Firkusny.

M: Stylistically speaking, where would you say Czech piano music could be placed?

F: Of course, we don't have so very much for the piano in Czech music. I think it's good music and should be played, and I was nursed on it. Smetana's writing was definitely influenced very much by Schumann, Liszt and Chopin. However, he wrote mostly polkas and dances, never a sonata or any of the major forms. Later he developed his own style, but the early compositions are very romantic. Dvorak is much more like Brahms, especially in his piano writing, which wasn't very idiomatic for the instrument. In his chamber music he is much more Brahmsian than Smetana, who is much closer to Schumann in many ways.

M: Are there any Czech concertos?

F: Only one: the Dvorak, and that is not his best work.

M: Do you play it?

F: Yes.

M: How long is the concerto?

F: Very long.

M: Have you ever taught it?

F: No. So far, nobody has asked to study it. Dvorak wrote this piano concerto when he was not yet very well-known. Shortly thereafter, he had great success in London. The concerto was published in Germany, but nobody played it. It was a completely forgotten piece. My piano teacher, Mr. Kurz, was a very fine pianist. When Kurz met Dvorak, they discussed his piano concerto. My teacher told Dvorak quite bluntly that it was not very well written for the piano, for it was not pianistic enough. Dvorak said

Of course, we don't have so very much for the piano in Czech music. I think it's good music and should be played, and I was nursed on it. Smetana's writing was definitely influenced very much by Schumann, Liszt and Chopin. However, he wrote mostly polkas and dances, never a sonata or any of the major forms. Later he developed his own style, but the early compositions are very romantic. . .Rudolf Firkusny.

jokingly, "Perhaps you would like to revise it." My teacher did; he made a more pianistic version. Dvorak died soon thereafter, so I don't know if he would have approved of it. I have played the concerto practically all my life, always trying to do something different. Finally, I decided to play the original, the unpianistic version by Dvorak. That was a hard job to relearn the piece because there are small differences, but I felt it was really much better.

M: I think it would be wonderful if you would play this music for our students at Juilliard. We are really not familiar with Czech music.

From having taught many students during the past years, what do you feel are the strong and weak points of students in general? What do you think they should concern themselves with?

F: That's hard for me to answer, because when students come to me, they are practically finished products, technically and pianistically. I try to do as little as possible because I don't want to take away their personalities and their feelings. I just try to advise them when I have the impression that they are not completely right, or not convincing. I try to see that they think more musically. Technique is very important, naturally, because without it we can't do anything, but it's not everything.

M: Do you feel that, in this day and age, we have too many of what I call "finger-pushers," who play only with their fingers, but don't use their imaginations in a creative, expressive way?

F: Yes, but there is a super-abundance of really fantastic talent. I don't remember anything like it before. Unfortunately, I think this emphasis on technical proficiency brings a certain uniformity. What I sometimes miss is a student who shows more individuality. This is difficult to find today.

When I heard something at a concert in Prague, I came home and played it. Then, somehow, Janácek heard about this curious child. He had a very bad reputation as a rather unpleasant and difficult man. When he wanted to hear me, many of my mother's friends discouraged her, saying, "Don't bring your child to that maniac!" But I wanted to go. . .Rudolf Firkusny.

102

M: I would like to initiate a different approach for young people who are ready to embark upon careers. Do you have any suggestions?

F: I think there are too many competitions, but I believe they are very important, because they give students stimulus and open up some broader possibilities.

M: But it spoils the competitiveness within oneself very often.

F: My idea has always been that a really big competition should take place approximately every three years and that several first prizes should be offered. At least three years, then, would be allowed to establish a student's career, after the initial recognition.

M: They are too young to have learned enough repertoire, let alone having had time for the experience of digesting it.

F: If you are that sensational, then you don't need competitions; you'll be found anyway. Michelangeli didn't win competitions, and he hasn't made a bad career. You need time to establish a career; you can't do it overnight. It's very easy to make a big splash, but what can you do after one year? Next year there is a new winner, and he is the hero.

M: I've been singularly fortunate in that many of my students have won competitions, but I still don't believe in them as the usual format stands now.

F: Frankly speaking, I have judged several competitions, and sometimes I have had the feeling that, although you have to give the prize to the one who is the all-around best, sometimes the one who *didn't* win has much more potential to develop into something great.

President Masaryk, as compensation for finishing all my studies, allowed me to leave Czechoslovakia for one year, so I went to Paris. I wanted to study with Cortot, but I did not work with him privately. I merely went to many classes, listened a lot, and attended all the concerts I possibly could. Cortot refused to teach me; I played for him and he told me that I didn't need a teacher, but a public. He engaged me to play in a concert which he conducted in Paris. . .Rudolf Firkusny.

M: Yes. They all need more time.

F: Often I tell my students, "If you're going to a competition, fine. It's a wonderful experience, but don't take it seriously if you don't make it. Sleep quietly."

M: Winning a competition is no guarantee that you will have or sustain a career; it takes much more than that. It is like launching a ship—it still has to sail.

F: If they keep the competitions going, there should be some financial support for longer preparation. Then, as I said, not only one prize, but at least three.

M: And why start in New York, the most challenging musical center? They should prepare repertoire for three or four years, and put things away. Not just have one Bach *prelude* and *Fugue*, one Mozart *sonata*, one Beethoven *sonata*, et cetera. New York, Boston, Philadelphia, London, Berlin, Vienna should come as the result of the prize and very much playing experience first, not vice versa!

F: In my career, I played in Czechoslovakia in the most unimportant little Lochs, which was wonderful. When I came here, I played God knows how many community concerts. It's the most wonderful experience you can have.

M: Rudolf, thank you again for the fascinating hour you have afforded us. I hope we can help to solve the problems and continue to guide some of these remarkably gifted young people with wisdom.

ALICIA de LARROCHA

Born in Barcelona, Alicia de Larrocha studied with the famous teacher Frank Marshall. Her career began modestly with recitals throughout her own country where Alfred Wallenstein heard her and invited her to appear with him and the Los Angeles Philharmonic. Since then, Madame de Larrocha has enjoyed an enormous success in concert and on recordings. Her reputation as an interpreter of Spanish keyboard music is only exceeded by the esteem in which she is held throughout the world by critics and audiences alike.

It is with the greatest pleasure that I submit some of the questions I posed to Mme. Alicia de Larrocha over breakfast at her hotel in New York City late in 1977. She did not wish to answer these questions immediately because she felt hesitant about expressing herself in English.

However, she allowed me to send these questions to her home in Barcelona, Spain, to be answered at her leisure in Spanish. Her responses have been translated. It is possible that some idiomatic phrases which she used have not been accurately conveyed in English. I do believe, however, that the essence is clearly stated. It was very interesting for me to have her agree to do this. Although we have been friends for many years, Mme. de Larrocha's acquiescence was a personal triumph because she dislikes interviews of any kind!

I admire Mme. de Larrocha enormously, not only as a very great artist, pianist, and musician who is completely dedicated to her work, but as a human being. The tremendous simplicity of approach as manifested in her playing communicates her total personality.

107

My first question was: "How do you study a new work and what are some of your initial approaches and practicing habits?" She answered: "If I am dealing with a work by a composer who is known to me, I go directly to the musical core and substance of what the composer seems to be telling me. I have never been fascinated by reading a work from beginning to end for the sole purpose of exploring the notes! Notes displease me when nothing is expressed! Furthermore, it is of utmost importance to find the proper fingering in order to facilitate an exact expression of the musical idea. At times, I have labored many years to achieve this."

"When the instrument or the acoustics of a hall do not respond to my interpretive wish, I have often changed fingerings during the concert itself, in order to obtain the accurate sound and character of a phrase I think essential. Sometimes, the fingering at that moment is not very orthodox but it does not matter."

"When I begin to learn a work totally unknown to me, I study it away from the piano first. After formulating an idea of the work in this manner, I then bring it to the piano and analyze everything at the instrument."

M: Alicia, do you memorize by harmonic analysis, by ear, by photographic memory, tactile sense, or all four? What do you depend upon most?

D: I believe all these ways are necessary and very important. However, none of them alone is sufficient. Most important for me is to study and analyze the form together with its harmonic and structural aspects. To review each section in my mind repeatedly is also very essential. Specific memorizing habits are frequently neglected, such as exact phrasings, agogics, dynamics, and absorbing as well as relating the rhythmic patterns. Important accents here and there can be an invaluable guide for the memory. I believe in studying and practicing each hand separately with all the foregoing ideas in mind and at extremely slow tempi.

When I begin to learn a work totally unknown to me, I study it away from the piano first. After formulating an idea of the work in this manner, I then bring it to the piano and analyze everything at the instrument. . .Alicia de Larrocha.

108

My first question was: "How do you study a new work and what are some of your initial approaches and practicing habits?" She answered: "If I am dealing with a work by a composer who is known to me, I go directly to the musical core and substance of what the composer seems to be telling me. I have never been fascinated by reading a work from beginning to end for the sole purpose of exploring the notes! Notes displease me when nothing is expressed! Furthermore, it is of utmost importance to find the proper fingering in order to facilitate an exact expression of the musical idea. At times, I have labored many years to achieve this.". . .Alicia de Laroccha.

There are some days when I feel like playing everything which constitutes technique: thirds, sixths, octaves and especially chords, Chopin etudes, etc. Other days, I am only attracted to simple works of pure music. My greatest obsession is to feel that my hands are flexible and firm at the same time. For this reason, without even being aware of it, I am always exercising the extension of my fingers, whether it is at the keyboard or on the top of a table, chair, any place. . .Alicia de Larrocha.

M: How have you managed to keep such a vast repertoire almost always at your fingertips? Do you go over old works periodically to keep them fresh in your memory?

D: My repertoire unfortunately is not as extensive as I wish it to be. I must confess that in my youth I did not work as much as I should have. However, the works I learned then I now retain easily. They require little review work. More recent pieces I have learned must be practiced consistently and conscientiously before each appearance.

M: What is your daily technical regimen, if any, like stretching exercises, etc.?

D: Since I am very irregular and variable with my life in general, my practicing habits are that way, too. There has never been what one might consider a consistent discipline in my work. What seems to have been most striking in my playing is a certain spontaneous intuition and impetus. I have never been able to explain this.

There are some days when I feel like playing everything which constitutes technique: thirds, sixths, octaves and especially chords, Chopin etudes, etc. Other days, I am only attracted to simple works of pure music. My greatest obsession is to feel that my hands are flexible and firm at the same time. For this reason, without even being aware of it, I am always exercising the extension of my fingers, whether it is at the keyboard or on the top of a table, chair, any place.

M: How do you practice the day of the concert? Do you practice much?

D: If I have a rehearsal with orchestra or must try out the piano, I do it in a reflective manner, and without giving of myself too much. I prefer to spare myself for the moment of the concert. If the piano has a heavy action, I work with a lot of weight in my fingers, and slowly. If the acoustics are poor and dry, I practice with the piano closed so that at the concert everything will sound better and easier. I almost always work without pedal. In this way, I search for legatos and sonorities which afterwards will be enriched with the pedal.

Of course, this is all relative since there are days when I have no time to try out the piano due to traveling; then there are other days in which I don't even want to see the piano before the concert.

When the instrument or the acoustics of a hall do not respond to my interpretive wish, I have often changed fingerings during the concert itself, in order to obtain the accurate sound and character of a phrase I think essential. Sometimes, the fingering at that moment is not very orthodox but it does not matter. . .Alicia de Larrocha.

It is very difficult to give advice. The only thing I can say is that in order to dedicate one's self to music, one has to consider it a true vocation and to love it, without setting any rigid conditions. The worst enemy of art is to be in a hurry. The command of an art is not achieved with a deadline in mind. A whole lifetime, no matter how long, is not enough to reach the goal of our ambitions. . . .Alicia de Larrocha.

musical america

1978 INTERNATIONAL DIRECTORY OF THE PERFORMING ARTS

Alicia de Larrocha
Musician of the Year

Reproduced here is the cover of **Musical America** *on which Alicia de Larrocha was featured as Musician of the Year.*

Since I am very irregular and variable with my life in general, my practicing habits are that way, too. There has never been what one might consider a consistent discipline in my work. What seems to have been most striking in my playing is a certain spontaneous intuition and impetus. I have never been able to explain this. . .Alicia de Larrocha.

M: Would you say a few things, Alicia, about tone, touch, phrasing, and pedaling? Do you feel that these are the keynotes to the distinctive pianistic, musical style?

D: All these factors, in my opinion, must go together to make a pianistic personality. The character and style of a work are given also by the sound. I believe every composer creates his character and atmosphere in sonority.

M: Do you think that we can separate sound from style?

D: I believe every style has to have its characteristic sound; thus, in my opinion, style and sound must never be separated. I also believe that sound has to be adjusted according to the tempo.

M: Would you please offer some suggestions to young people regarding the need for discipline, total dedication, and patience? Whatever you feel and say will mean so much.

D: It is very difficult to give advice. The only thing I can say is that in order to dedicate one's self to music, one has to consider it a true vocation and to love it, without setting any rigid conditions. The worst enemy of art is to be in a hurry. The command of an art is not achieved with a deadline in mind. A whole lifetime, no matter how long, is not enough to reach the goal of our ambitions.

M: Thank you very much, Alicia de Larrocha. It has been a great honor to hear your comments and to interview you; I know that your words will reverberate in many countries and will be cherished by all.

Schubert is a composer, along with Mozart, with whom I have not felt comfortable in public. I feel immensely at home with Schubert in private. However, I believe that Schubert is really not for a 3,000 seat concert hall. His music has an intimacy that invites playing for your good friends, just because you love his music. . . . Garrick Ohlsson.

GARRICK OHLSSON

Since winning the Chopin International Piano Competition in Warsaw in 1970, Garrick Ohlsson has firmly established himself as one of the leading young pianists in the concert world today. Born in White Plains, New York, Ohlsson came to the Juilliard School to study with Sascha Gorodnitski at the age of thirteen. He later went on to study with Madame Rosina Lhevinne and others. His playing is characterized by clean lines and lucidity and he eschews a percussive and mechanistic approach to the keyboard. He has recorded extensively on both the Angel and Connoisseur Society labels and is known throughout Europe and the Far East for the extraordinary refinement of his playing.

Marcus: Since the auspicious launching of your career, and the equally significant continuation of it, in what ways have you evolved, vis-à-vis your approach to music in general and its performance in particular?

Ohlsson: That's a very big and many-faceted question: I'll tackle it one part at a time. In very practical terms, I cannot do now what I did when I was a student. For example, to begin my day practicing Beethoven's *Sonata, Op. 110,* and just continue to go over the music for several hours without arriving at any specific decisions would be impossible today! Now I must be very pragmatic about what I'm learning. "Do I know the notes, dynamics, phrasing, and many infinite details?" In other words, what am I learning? Then I put it to bed for a while.

Naturally, I play a great deal each season, and therefore a lot of my study must be done away from the piano. I begin to work on the music mentally, so that I can evolve a more personal approach. This mental involvement and fine-honing has given me a greater precision in determining what the music actually says to me. I feel more intensely committed to what I ultimately decide to do. Prior to this, I felt very confused and could not find my own direction.

121

M: I'm sure that you have much more of a choice now, and that choice is exciting rather than confusing.

O: Absolutely. The more I learn, the more options I have in any situation—both musically and personally. I feel that having more choices and more ideas when you sit down to practice is, as you say, immensely exciting.

M: Then you're able to establish and solidify your personal convictions about a piece of music both at the keyboard and away from it.

O: But very much away! For me that's very important. In my student days, when I gave a few performances each year, each one was a life and death event. It was a real struggle. I threw all my musical and emotional eggs into one basket, and sometimes it went well, sometimes it did not. We have all experienced this. But on the good side of performing a great deal, one becomes so routined that each performance is viewed not as a symbol of the ultimate achievement, but as something integrated into your normal life. In other words, you are not living your entire life so that, at the end of six months, you can get up on stage and play. You are living so that you can function as an artist and musician, and lead a normal life in music. Performance does not become a freakish commitment, but rather something you want to do, and with regularity.

M: Your calendar doesn't stop with each performance!

O: Exactly! On the other side, there is always that danger of either getting too tired or too routined, so that you lose a certain spark or vitality. This can happen to anybody for any number of reasons. But, for me, that's one of the greatest dangers.

M: What do you do, let us say, when you are inordinately tired, and understandably so, with travel, new halls, new hotels, new people, new pianos, new everything? What do you find advantageous to revitalize your enthusiasm for music?

O: It depends on how good or bad I feel. First of all, I make sure that I do get enough rest. This is extremely important. The emotions function within the physical body, which is a fact nobody seems to have acknowledged yet. If one does not feel very well, then nothing looks good, not even the piano. When I am on the road and happen to have a free day, one of the most salutary things I can do is to dig into some beautiful music I love, not necessarily anything I am currently playing. When one is playing publicly a

122

lot, there is little time to do anything but polish the material one has to perform. Although you are playing familiar literature, still it is one program tonight, and in two days a different one, then a concerto. You are constantly running through things. But for me, an important thing is to sit down at the piano and spend a morning with a Chopin *nocturne* I love, or some part of a sonata, and feel refreshed.

M: To fall in love with music so that you can recapture a mood.

O: Yes, absolutely. That mood is extremely important. It's a many-faceted mood, but it's basically one of excitement and infatuation. Then when I go out on stage, I feel more communicative and inspired.

M: Do you ever feel that you love a certain composer, and yet sometimes hesitate to program his music?

O: Absolutely!

M: Can you say why, or cite a composition that you may have loved and still reserve the right to say, "No, not yet; maybe later?"

O: Let me theorize for a moment. I believe that a talented child will play best that which has been taught to him out of the teacher's strongest conviction and sympathy. In my own case, my early teachers concentrated on what we call the great Romantic literature, which means very roughly the period from the end of Mozart's life until the beginning of World War I. Since ninety percent of the music I played came from that period, I imagine that I felt the most comfortable in that area. Of course, that's an enormous period —the greatest in piano literature. That's saying a lot. Now I'm not even sure that I am always the most comfortable within that framework. For the past eight or nine years, I've had a hangup about Mozart. Having played a good deal of Chopin, Liszt, Rachmaninoff, Brahms, Schumann, and Beethoven, I became accustomed to the technical challenges: lots of notes and rich tonal sounds. Generally, I enjoyed the extremes of big fortissimos and pianissimos. The extremes, when one is very young, represent the tremendous joy of playing the piano. When you approach Mozart, you approach the peak of great composition, as it were; one cannot help him very much. His music is so complete, perfect, and ravishing that one cannot listen to what one is doing without feeling taken over by the wonder of it all!

M: I think that you've said a great deal, because I remember years

There are a couple of words of consolation which, as I get more experienced, I would like to pass on. As to pianists and hands: because I have a huge hand, I should have no sympathy for the problems of the hands, but I have immense interest in what hands do. I am concerned with what emotionally-charged students do, students who believe that by making everything important, they will be successful and in the end make nothing important. Those of us who have any sort of flair or temperament for the keyboard, at one time or other, try too hard. Most of the time I feel the hand is almost too powerful for the piano. In most cases, we don't have to kill the darned instrument. I find that when the greatest pianists are playing, especially the ones who impress you with their climaxes, they are working within a very subtle range of color. Horowitz has, between piano and pianissimo at least five more degrees than most pianists. He gets up to forte, and it sounds really impressive. . . . Garrick Ohlsson.

124

ago someone said, "Mozart is the height of sophistication." This was comparable to the analogy of someone climbing a mountain; the mountain of life, let us say. First, we absorb one view and, going further, another, the third and fourth views, et cetera. Finally, in reaching the summit, we have collected many views of life, and very often we return to the simplicity of our first view. By then, however, it is not childish simplicity, but the pure, child-like simplicity of maturity.

O: I would say that, at some point during every year, I review a Mozart sonata or concerto. It is always a rewarding experience from which I learn and feel enriched.

As I get older, I find that planning programs becomes more interesting and easier. Variety is so important, experience gives me a wider choice.

M: Yes. I think choice is a very important thing in all aspects of study, as long as one's groundwork is solid. If one, when young, is exposed to certain composers which show him in the most felicitous light, then, as you aptly said, the personality develops and the variegated palette takes over.

At this point, do you follow a technical routine, or don't you bother with that?

O: I love the way you phrase that! At this point in my career, I don't really follow a technical routine. I do a great deal of technical work within the music, but I've always done that. I have not really paid much attention to scales and that sort of drillwork since I was about twelve. However, as I said, I practice many ways where pianistic things are concerned.

M: You work in every possible way in order to assure the necessary security?

O: As far as possible, absolutely. And the artistic sensibilities come into technical things, too. They are so related that it's impossible to divide them.

M: Of course, pianism is motivated by the music itself. With a technical equipment as extensive and comprehensive as yours, do you ever encounter certain types of pianistic hurdles that bug you? I have found people who have ten fabulous fingers and yet, somehow, trills, skips, and broken octaves, for example, seem to bug them. Are you immune to all of that? I would guess you are!

O: I seem to be endowed for the instrument. I've worked at it very hard and it's fascinating, but the basic building blocks were healthy and solid. I have not met big challenges which I couldn't solve. One thing, however, speaking in all candor, which pianists who have a natural pianistic potential somehow find difficult or neglect, is in the piano-pianissimo range. It seems easy to play it flat and lifeless. This is a big thing which has bugged me, and I'm working extremely hard on it; to be able to retain quality, life, and beauty in the tone. With pianissimo, it's all right, because somehow that whisper is exciting, if true. But a really beautiful piano sound is something that I find in few pianists, actually, don't you?

M: An expressive tone, yes. You just anticipated my next question: how do you practice for a deeper, wider, tonal palette? What music would you suggest to a student as helpful toward developing a deeper tone, with more color, and, of course, expressivity?

O: There are several sides to this from which I work. One is technical, which is the least satisfactory for something expressive. The other side is totally human. I sincerely believe that the pianist must *create* tone; the sound is already there, and is relatively pleasant, but you must draw it out of the piano, and you must free it. There are many ways to do this. One tone, of course, is meaningless by itself; it's the relationship between tones that counts.

M: Don't you sometimes feel that, when you conjure up one sound at the beginning of a piece, it will set the mood for you as well as for the listener?

O: That's critically important. Sometimes you go to a performance and you know from the first sound what the end is going to be. There are a number of ways of beginning, of course, which we all get very nervous about. . .

M: That's part of the routine like brushing your teeth every day.

O: But we must begin. First of all, beginning any piece is a great declaration of faith, because why should we break the silence? In order to break the silence, I feel that one must generate the music within oneself. If it's a Beethoven sonata which begins with vigor, sometimes I will recollect how he gets back into it after the recapitulation, and inside myself, I'll play four or five bars. If I'm playing the Tchaikovsky *Concerto*, where there is a lot of thunder in the beginning, I play the orchestra part within myself, even when practicing . . . make a tremendous crescendo toward my opening chords.

126

In my student days, when I gave a few performances each year, each one was a life and death event. It was a real struggle. I threw all my musical and emotional eggs into one basket, and sometimes it went well, sometimes it did not. We have all experienced this. But on the good side of performing a great deal, one becomes so routined that each performance is viewed not as a symbol of the ultimate achievement, but as something integrated into your normal life. In other words, you are not living your entire life so that, at the end of six months, you can get up on stage and play. You are living so that you can function as an artist and musician, and lead a normal life in music. Performance does not become a freakish commitment, but rather something you want to do, and with regularity. . .Garrick Ohlsson.

127

M: Creating the music within yourself means there is an inner singing, pulse, and momentum where the emotions are immediately involved and set free. At this point, what you are expressing is your chief concern and the piano becomes malleable—not to play at but to use as an adjunct.

O: Absolutely. You don't play at the piano, you make the piano your collaborator. The piano sits there, a formidable challenge, but it's what you do with it that's most important. Everybody is a marvelous pianist today; it's getting to be quite worrisome. However, rarely do we hear someone who makes the piano become human. How to do that becomes a lifetime's work, I suppose.

M: Do you feel that music should sing or speak?

O: And dance, too. The singing aspect is often neglected, although we all pay lip-service to it at one time or another.

M: Don't you sing when you practice?

O: Surely; that's very important. The musical impulse originally arises from song and dance, and speaking gives it uni-significance, either in a big dramatic context or a small one. Beethoven *speaks* a lot. The dialogues sometimes fight with each other, but when they sing together, it's a miracle.

M: When a phrase doesn't meet with your artistic approval, what do you do to change it? Naturally, you cannot generalize about a phrase. Many years ago someone said to me, "How do you phrase?" Now, that's ridiculous! It is like saying, "How do you make a sentence?" But what are your working habits? Given the underlying emotion and meaning which it generates—the style, color, shape, dynamics, pedal, et cetera. If you try very hard to put it all together and if you do not succeed do you put it off for another day, or stick to it?

There are three composers who continually obsess me: Chopin, Liszt and Schubert. I love Chopin for his incredible, unparalleled pianistic intuition, his lucidity and the way he copes with the most sophisticated, demoniac, sensuous, and mad feelings that you can experience. He puts them into such a classical context that they become lucid and unconfused. He truly is a classicist—so focused—and this appeals to me. . . . Garrick Ohlsson.

O: I'm generally a "stick-to-it" person, although there are times when you simply have to say: "Today is not the day for this." Generally, I try to look at the music and gain a mental idea of how it sounds, but that's very general. A composer writes every note, and if you are an artist, you have to have some kind of relationship with just about every note in the piece; otherwise, it can't become yours. Some of the notes are more important than others. Sometimes young students who have a great emotional gift try to make everything important and as a result, nothing is important. Without a sense of proportion, you lose contrast and balance. You do all the analytical things: "Where's the high point of the phrase? What is the relationship of the melody to the bass line? What's your pedal doing? Do you actually have any idea of what your pedal is doing? Pedaling is one of those things we're very intuitive about.

M: But you are very specific about pedaling when you finally polish a work?

O: Yes, Im getting much more so. The pedal can make not only combinations of sounds, but it can also phrase for you, especially in the bass. It can give your playing immense power, as I'm discovering now.

M: The sonority of the harmonic structure sustains the melodic line.

O: The pedal is becoming very fascinating to me now. I knew at some point it would. I've been discussing the pedal with a few Russian pianists, and I've been surprised at the time they spend experimenting with it. Ashkenazy says that he spends fully one-quarter of his time paying attention to what his right foot is doing.

M: It is an art in itself and yet totally related to everything we play. How do you feel about Bach? Do you think that people should sit with their feet under the pedals as though they were typing and just play all the notes as articulately as possible?

O: Oh good God, no. Who wants to listen to that? If you're going to play Bach on the piano, which I suppose is not historically correct, then do it as he would if he had had the modern piano. Bach played all instruments very well; therefore I refuse to believe that, had he encountered our modern pianos, he would not want to experiment with pedals.

M: I'm sure you're right. You say something which is very close

130

First of all, beginning any piece is a great declaration of faith, because why should we break the silence? In order to break the silence, I feel that one must generate the music within oneself. If it's a Beethoven sonata which begins with vigor, sometimes I will recollect how he gets back into it after the recapitulation, and inside myself, I'll play four or five bars. If I'm playing the Tchaikovsky Concerto, where there is a lot of thunder in the beginning, I play the orchestra part within myself, even when practicing . . . make a tremendous crescendo toward my opening chords . . . Garrick Ohlsson.

131

*Let me theorize for a moment. I believe that a
talented child will play best that which has been
taught to him out of the teacher's strongest
conviction and sympathy. In my own case, my early
teachers concentrated on what we call the great
Romantic literature, which means very roughly the
period from the end of Mozart's life until the
beginning of World War I. Since ninety percent of the
music I played came from that period, I imagine that
I felt the most comfortable in that area. Of course,
that's an enormous period —the greatest in piano
literature. . .Garrick Ohlsson.*

132

to my heart. Bach, who was such a genius, would not ignore the modern facilities for making music that he would have at his disposal.

How do you memorize? Do you memorize consciously first? In our profession, time is of the essence and I'm sure you memorize quickly and easily.

O: Now, I've begun to memorize much more immediately. Previously, it was one of those things which happened automatically. It still happens more or less automatically, depending upon my familiarity with the work, if I have the work "in my ears."

M: Do you think of structural analysis, harmonic analysis?

O: To a certain extent. Harmonic analysis is very important, especially for the harmonic quirks in any phrase or section of a piece. When I work at a piece, I often memorize immediately, and work each hand separately. If I have very little time, I'll play a four- or eight-bar phrase, close the music, and try it from memory. If it doesn't work, I ask myself, "What haven't I learned yet?" I analyze it by ear. (I have perfect pitch, but that's no great gift; half the world has it.) Then I analyze the piece by digital or tactile memory, which I find very important. The visual memory generally doesn't work quite as well for me. I know people who can enter your apartment for five minutes, leave, and two days later tell you every object, its color, et cetera, in the room; I'm not one of those people. Ear memory is very acute with me. Memorizing the voice leading I sometimes find very useful. Brahms and Rachmaninoff are two excellent contrapuntalists, and very acute. If memorizing a Rachmaninoff work becomes troublesome what with six-note chords and complicated inner voices, analyzing those inner voices helps to understand the melodic line, and why he wrote it the way he did.

M: I remember years ago someone said that when you're very young, you play with all of your virtuoso enthusiasm; when you're middle-aged, you play with all of your musicianship; and when you get much, much older, you look for the inner voices.

O: Then maybe I can retire soon!

M: Hardly! What do you feel is the difference between recording a work and performing it publicly?

O: Basically, I very much prefer performing in public.

M: Why?

I'm generally a "stick-to-it" person, although there are times when you simply have to say: "Today is not the day for this." Generally, I try to look at the music and gain a mental idea of how it sounds, but that's very general. A composer writes every note, and if you are an artist, you have to have some kind of relationship with just about every note in the piece; otherwise, it can't become yours. Some of the notes are more important than others . . . Garrick Ohlsson.

134

O: Because I enjoy the spontaneous involvement between me and the music, and the ideas I can communicate to the audience. In recording, I feel uneasy with all the mechanical equipment and the possibility of missing a few notes.

M: Does it inhibit you in your interpretive spontaneity?

O: Yes, I feel it does. It restricts one's flights of fantasy. It is hard to get carried away in a studio where all devices are geared for precision, and the technological considerations dampen your mood.

M: It's a very special challenge. Indeed, there is sometimes a bigger accuracy of musical message in live performance.

O: As far as recording accuracy is concerned, they can fix up smudged notes remarkably. I recall, in recording Chopin's *Prelude in B-flat minor*, there were inevitable splices which had to be done. None of us is quite perfect enough to play it, except perhaps Josef Lhevinne.

M: He played it remarkably, but he played it his entire life!

O: Now when something is spliced, (and theoretically, if you play the piece over and over again, eventually you do strike all the right notes), they can't fix just one note; they must splice a section, a bar, two bars, or a phrase. Believe me, to start a phrase in the midst of a climactic passage just tears your guts out; you get hysterical!

M: In addition, you find that the piano you adored on stage does not always sound best in the recording studio. That becomes another hurdle!

O: Absolutely. All these things do, and everything's magnified.

M: How do you manage to keep a considerable repertoire going when you are on tour, when practicing facilities are not always available to you?

O: You've touched upon something which is disagreeable to all pianists. Generally, on tour, you try to make arrangements to practice somewhere at a convenient time. First, it invariably takes an hour of aggravation to get there, and you frequently find the place closed. You manage to ring somebody's bell and wake him up. Then he wants to listen a bit. The piano hasn't been tuned, the lighting is poor, it's cold or hot, there's not a chair that is within six inches of the right height. All these things to contend with, yet somehow we manage! Then, after about a half hour of work, you find nothing is going anywhere. At home, you can read a book,

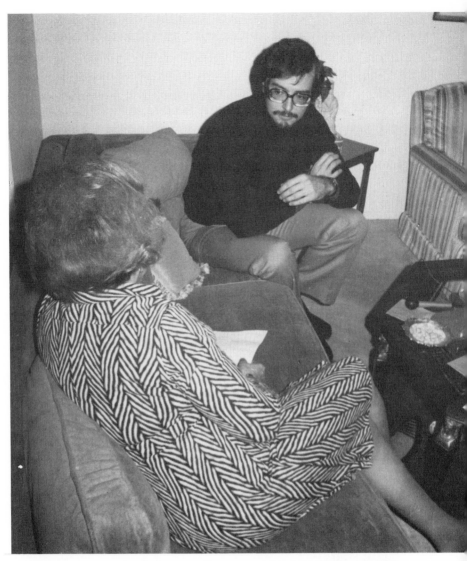

In very practical terms, I cannot do now what I did when I was a student. For example, to begin my day practicing Beethoven's Sonata, Op. 110, *and just continue to go over the music for several hours without arriving at any specific decisions would be impossible today! Now, I must be very pragmatic about what I'm learning. "Do I know the notes, dynamics, phrasing, and many infinite details?" In other words, what am I learning? Then I put it to bed for a while. . .Garrick Ohlsson.*

make a phone call, or go for a walk and come back in an hour to try again. On tour, you haven't that option. Other instrumentalists who travel with their own instruments are much luckier.

M: Years ago, when I was living in Dallas with my husband, Isaac Stern visited our city. We called him late one night, and he said he was practicing. I said, "How and where can you practice so late?" He said, "With my mute on in the bathroom, and I'm practically asphyxiated!"

O: Another frequent happening is that you find repair men attending to stage matters when you get to the hall, and the place hasn't been cleaned for the performance. Then you proceed to rehearse your program through an unbelievable clatter of noise.

M: And quiet is so essential!

O: You have to work on the very pieces that you're going to play because of the new acoustics and a different piano. Also, you must check whether the pedals work; whether they squeak, or one is about to fall off, or some other disturbing situation.

This is more common than you might think. Then the unevenness in the keyboard itself must be analyzed to determine which notes you have to remember to play slightly less or slightly more.

M: These are the unforeseen obstacles. Then, of course, you must also practice the new pieces scheduled for three weeks later! I remember a conversation with Rudolf Serkin at Mrs. Leventritt's home many years ago. He was telling a young pianist the following: "When you go on tour, never think that you're going to have time to practice; forget it. The three hours that you have scheduled in your mind to practice the forthcoming concerto never materialize." It's like a mirage in the desert: when you get there, it is not visible. Those three hours have been taken up either by an interview, a television show, or radio broadcast. This is why I ask someone like you, who plays so many concerts. . .

O: I do about ninety this season!

M: That's being on stage almost every third day. In the old days, they did not play that much. Mr. Horowitz told me that he never accepted summer engagements. Josef Lhevinne would practice his new programs from the end of May until the end of September. At any rate, we know what inhuman schedules some artists fulfill.

O: The younger you are, the more easily you'll accept a bizarre travel schedule.

S-387

138

M: What happens during the periods away from any public appearances or recording?

O: You've already pushed my pleasure button!

M: What literature do you turn to quite naturally? What satisfies you, allows you to express emotionally, technically what you feel? What shows you in the most felicitous light?

O: There are three composers who continually obsess me in this way: Chopin, Liszt and Schubert. I love Chopin for his incredible, unparalleled pianistic intuition, his lucidity and the way he copes with the most sophisticated, demoniac, sensuous, and mad feelings that you can experience. He puts them into such a classical context that they become lucid and unconfused. He truly is a classicist—so focused—and this appeals to me.

I love the grandeur of Liszt: the theater, the great drama, and even the religion in him. His music is not piano music per se, yet he is the other colossal piano composer to be ranked with Chopin. The piano becomes opera, orchestra, and declamation of speech. It is the total grandeur of a very big and generous man.

Schubert is a composer, along with Mozart, with whom I have not felt comfortable in public. I feel immensely at home with Schubert in private. However, I believe that Schubert is really not for a 3,000 seat concert hall. His music has an intimacy that invites playing for your good friends, just because you love his music.

M: That is the way he was. There is always a man behind the music.

O: A very gentle man, and I happen to have a tremendously soft spot for him. I love all kinds of music. I certainly love to fight with Beethoven, but don't we all? Also, I am fascinated with contemporary music and have not devoted enough time to it. To do justice to a contemporary piece, one probably should spend more time, rather than less, on it whereas most of us feel that we can get away with it in less time.

I love the grandeur of Liszt: the theater, the great drama, and even the religion in him. His music is not piano music per se, yet he is the other colossal piano composer to be ranked with Chopin. The piano becomes opera, orchestra, and declamation of speech. It is the total grandeur of a very big and generous man. . . . Garrick Ohlsson.

I seem to be endowed for the instrument. I've worked at it very hard and it's fascinating, but the basic building blocks were healthy and solid. I have not met big challenges which I couldn't solve. One thing, however, speaking in all candor, which pianists who have a natural pianistic potential somehow find difficult or neglect, is in the piano-pianissimo range. It seems easy to play it flat and lifeless. This is a big thing which has bugged me, and I'm working extremely hard on it; to be able to retain quality, life, and beauty in the tone. With pianissimo, it's all right, because somehow that whisper is exciting, if it's true. But a really beautiful piano sound is something that I find in few pianists . . . Garrick Ohlsson.

140

M: So many people try to hide behind the newness of it, feeling that it won't be understood anyway.

O: There is a heck of a lot of charlatanism in that particular attitude.

M: But I think that you're definitely one of those who would want to make it more interesting and bring out the subtleties of it.

O: I hope so.

M: I remember your wonderful performance of *Gaspard de la Nuit*, particularly *Scarbo*, years ago, and how you managed to get the whole feeling of the piece. Do you play much French music?

O: Not very much, but I love French music.

M: It's a question of time, isn't it?

O: Right now, it is. If I had the time, I probably would play everything, at least for myself. There are a couple of words of consolation which, as I get more experienced, I would like to pass on. As to pianists and hands: because I have a huge hand, I should have no sympathy for the problems of the hands, but I have immense interest in what hands do. I am concerned with what emotionally-charged students do, students who believe that by making everything important, they will be successful and in the end make nothing important. Those of us who have any sort of flair or temperament for the keyboard, at one time or other, try too hard. Most of the time I feel the hand is almost too powerful for the piano. In most cases, we don't have to kill the darned instrument. I find that when the greatest pianists are playing, especially the ones who impress you with their climaxes, they are working within a very subtle range of color. Horowitz has, between piano and pianissimo, at least five more degrees than most pianists. He gets up to forte, and it sounds really impressive. Then when he really lets out, "Boy oh boy oh boy!" Let's face it: he's not beating his brains out most of the time, which is what we tend to want to do. This is just a word of encouragement I'd like to give to most people who think that if they try harder, if they force themselves more. . . piano-playing is not weight-lifting. It's more like dancing, or gymnastics.

M: Forcing is one of the most dangerous things in the world. At all levels, the piano should have a sonority which projects without a hammered forearm approach. You draw it out, it doesn't come from the fingers. In playing the violin, the more pressure you give from the bow-arm, the more tone you have. You still have the firm tactile feeling on the string or key, whether you play pianissimo or forte. It's the same thing; you still have to play deeply into the key to play softly, but you give less weight, that's all.

O: The string is struck by the hammer and must resound and vibrate freely, whereas many pianists play it as if they would hit a bell, and would keep the clapper on the bell the moment they struck it, which would kill the sound, rather than letting it ring and be free. As you say, drawing forth the sound, rather than hammering it into the keyboard.

M: You draw a bow across the strings; you don't push the music into the violin, you draw it out. The prospect of seeing pianists draw sound out of the piano, instead of pushing sound into the piano where the sound is already, would make my life very, very happy. But of course it's very difficult, because you have an ivory or plastic key, a hard surface, and while you say, "Dig deeply into the bed of the piano," the piano has no bed. But you should try at least to release your weight so that it will follow through. The last finger joint must be firm and developed.

O: Of course, this is a very complicated subject, and one on which we spend our whole lives working.

M: Exactly, but I think that young people don't realize that they don't spend enough time on that craft. This has to do with your personal relationship to the way you play, the way you feel music, and what you really want to express.

O: We never want that kind of hammered sound, unless it's on purpose. Once in a while, maybe one percent of the time, you're going to want a really sharp, hard sound. If you're going to do that, you'd better want it, and not do it just because you don't know how to do anything else.

M: Exactly. And there's even a way to do that, so that it can be very bitey, sardonic, and sarcastic, but it still is not hitting the piano.

O: I believe that everything is permissible; as you say, play it with your left foot if it helps. I am so sick of methods at this point, and of people who play only with the tips of the fingers, or only on the cushions, et cetera . . . it all works together. You can play from almost any joint in your body, and combine them in the most wonderful ways.

142

M: You can, after you really know *one* way to play. Then you can break all the rules intelligently. If you break them intelligently, then everything is feasible and permissible. Thank you, Garrick. This has been most informative and exceedingly enjoyable. I look forward with great pleasure to hearing one of your concerts soon.

You don't play at the piano, you make the piano your collaborator. The piano sits there, a formidable challenge, but it's what you do with it that's most important. Everybody is a marvelous pianist today; it's getting to be quite worrisome. However, rarely do we hear someone who makes the piano become human. How to do that becomes a lifetime's work, I suppose . . . Garrick Ohlsson.

The modern instruments are becoming less and less good. We remember the pre-war pianos, which usually were good or great. We are now confronted with instruments which range from dreadful to great. When one is compelled to play on a piano with hammers that are steely and edgy, the worst thing one can do is to strike the key fast. The best thing one can do is to pull the sound out. I remember Josef and Rosina Lhevinne saying to both of us, "You must approach the piano like a lover, not like an enemy." Don't hit it; stroke it. Pull the sound out slowly, and with depth. . . . John Browning.

JOHN BROWNING

Equally at home in eighteenth-century classical music, nineteenth-century romantic music, or contemporary avant-garde music, John Browning is recognized internationally as a true virtuoso of the keyboard. A frequent guest with orchestras throughout the world, Browning made his piano debut at the age of ten, but concedes that he did not begin to perform "professionally" until he was twenty.

Marcus: John, your studying habits have always intrigued me, primarily because you are not only a fast, thorough learner, but there is such a searching intelligence behind all your responses. What is your normal procedure in studying a new work?

Browning: My normal approach would be to read straight through the work quickly. In that way, I would get an idea of where the problems lie and where the repetitions are, which obviously, for memory purposes, are valuable. To grasp the emotion of the piece and its general scope, I would read it straight through. Then I would go back, and from experience I have learned that it is best to do the places first which are not obviously difficult. In other words, I would possibly memorize the slow movement or less difficult sections, where finger memory won't work. I would memorize the non-tactile things first, and then the tactile things. Frequently, I do the old "four measures with and four measures without," or a page with, a page without the music, and then interlock. Adele, I think you also were saying something about going to the cadence, and then returning to two measures before the cadence, and proceeding to the next section. In other words, never leave a seam until you have closed back on it.

M: That's a very good analogy. Are you saying that you memorize a work the moment you begin to study it?

B: There are things that will stick in my mind immediately, therefore there are things that I know. This is perhaps why I memorize the non-obvious things first, because the obvious things are automatically fixed in my mind. The structural difficulties re-

quire more study, and I don't know whether they can be determined by one reading. If you are a very mature musician, yes, they could be. Many times, these problems are not apparent until the second, third, or later readings.

M: Yes, definitely. How do you work when you have brought a piece to the level of a real performance, where many details have been explored? Do you ever change your initial conception? This is an involved question.

B: Very! Perhaps that is the crux question of all, because this is where the artist keeps going back into himself to reach his own level, and what he really thinks and feels about the composition. When I suddenly realize that it doesn't feel or sound right and I can't explain why, I almost automatically, as a formula, strip the entire thing; I go right back to point one. I start from the beginning of the work, with the score, and relearn it.

M: When you change it, what are some of the things you do?

B: I rarely change fingerings; in fact, most of my scores are unfingered. Sometimes I'm sorry about that, because if I take up a work years after I played it, I regret not having marked down the fingerings. Where the music itself is concerned: if something isn't making sense to me, either from my brain, ears, or heart, then I review the score again, because I feel somehow I will get a clue from that. Something will tell me from the score.

M: I am sure you feel that the score dictates and motivates everybody's interpretation, because that's the source, and you have to keep on searching for the validity of your convictions.

B: Except that we're like archaeologists; the source is not totally reliable. We still have to use our own intuitions.

M: There is a wonderful Talmudic quotation which says, "If you want to understand the invisible, you must study very carefully the visible."

To grasp the emotion of the piece and its general scope, I would read it straight through. Then I would go back, and from experience I have learned that it is best to do the places first which are not obviously difficult. In other words, I would possibly memorize the slow movement or less difficult sections, where finger memory won't work. . . . John Browning.

147

When you have already used all of your artistic sensibilities and have performed a work to your own satisfaction, how do you re-evaluate it when you return to it at a later date? You certainly don't try to recapture what you did before.

B: Never; that's the worst thing you can do, because *you* have changed. This is why you must use the "strip" method; strip away all of your old ideas and start as though you were learning the work from scratch.

M: Sometimes don't you feel that what you are doing may be the direct antithesis of what you've done before?

B: Yes, very often. However, the old expression, "All roads lead to Rome," can be revised to mean, "There are many ways of getting to Rome." You may have gotten there five years ago via one method, but that may not work for you now. You have to find another way to get to the same place; not necessarily aiming for a different performance, but altering your previous approach so that it still satisfies your sincerest convictions.

M: I think re-learning a great work is a real challenge; to find new depths, to broaden one's meaning and find a direction which may have escaped us years earlier.

Where do you feel the younger generation of gifted pianists show their limitations?

B: As my ancestor would have said, "Let me count the ways." My main objection to many young pianists is, first of all, their approach to the keyboard. They don't dig into the bottom of the keys. As we both know, having worked with Josef Lhevinne, that was something he used to stress time and time again: "Get to the bottom of the key!" I feel that the ego-trip of the young is one of their biggest stumbling blocks. We love them because they are talented, attractive, eager, and ambitious, but when it comes to the art, they are so involved with love—but they don't know what love means yet! They're in love with the act of making music, rather than with the music itself. One performs because one loves music, not because one must perform. To be out on stage before 3,000 people should not be the reason.

M: You mean that the dedication to the study of great and interesting music necessitates our real love. The process must be rewarding, as well as the goal. I believe it all has to do with the speed with which everybody wants to evolve a career. In other

148

words, the studying processes do not include first a real craft, then the art. This is the difficulty. They want to get to what is on top—the icing, the art—and try to project that, so that they can step quickly onto the stage. This bothers me very much.

B: You use the word that I believe is crucial: craft. One must know one's craft. This is a word nobody uses anymore, because it involves discipline, self-analysis, examination, and hard work. To me, we are not floating in the clouds; we are craftsmen.

M: In order to become an artist, I feel, one has to know one's craft as a basis for everything one does interpretively.

B: The craft, in fact, means understanding the art so well that one allows everything. It is only the uninformed who are rigid and who put down little tight rules.

M: What I generally tell my students is that one must know the rules very well before one can break them intelligently. If the craftsmanship is so secure, experienced, and multi-faceted, our interpretations can afford to reach both the heights and depths of our imaginative insights.

B: I like to feel that, if I explore everything, then I'm really functioning from knowledge and not from stupidity.

M: I would like to discuss with you the whimsical approaches to interpretation that we find substituting for concepts. The current campaign for freedom can effectively destroy the sense of taste,

Most students pedal the way one drives a car: they simply put their foot on the accelerator. The more they press down on it, the faster they go. They do not understand pedal as an instrument of color and, as Lhevinne said, "the soul of the piano." Without the pedal, we have no piano. The pedal has so many depths. In playing Mozart, I almost never use full pedal, but I almost never use "no pedal." I use a small degree of pedal which keeps the sound alive, warm, and liquid, but does not interfere with the passagework. . . . John Browning.

style, and meaning. An oratorical recitative of Bach can suddenly sound like a flowery phrase by Fauré rather than the healthy, full-blooded, original utterance.

B: I do think that the reverent approach in playing Mozart, for example, can lead to a "daintiness" which I don't especially like and certainly don't find appropriate. After all, one need only skim through Mozart's letters as translated by Emily Anderson to find an abundance of earthy, four-lettered words intermingled with the musings of an eighteenth-century mind. We see that, far from being a dainty man, Mozart was a very earthy one with a kind of earthiness, as one finds in *Le Nozze di Figaro*, that even the nobility could accept. The commoner who wasn't noble recognized the need to develop taste. Taste was not an overlay; it was visceral, something important. It was not the frosting, as you said earlier; it was the cake itself. It was where the substance was. So often, students do things whimsically without the slightest awareness of what they are doing. Their discipline has not yet reached the point where they can see the difference between the real value and the whim. Their musical values have not matured enough to distinguish between the important and the unimportant.

M: And I'm sure you feel that if everything is important, then nothing is important. What are your thoughts on building mechanics, technique, and ultimately, an advanced pianism? Let us say from the elementary and intermediate students to the most advanced?

I do think that the reverent approach in playing Mozart, for example, can lead to a "daintiness" which I don't especially like and certainly don't find appropriate. After all, one need only skim through Mozart's letters as translated by Emily Anderson to find an abundance of earthy, four-lettered words intermingled with the musings of an eighteenth-century mind. . . . John Browning.

If we take Josef Lhevinne's statement: "The pedal is the soul of the piano," one step further, we must think as intensively about the pedal as we would about our spiritual life. Not too many young people do, which is unfortunate. . . . John Browning.

152

B: Being by nature a disciplined person, I am completely convinced of the need for a daily regimen. However, as disciplined as it must be, the daily routine need not always be rigidly adhered to; it can become comparable to a blind ritual or a superstition. One does not always have to begin with scales or exercises. Should a piano not be available, there are other ways of studying. Many times I go to the piano after very little sleep and a rather rough night, and I play Bach fugues. Another day, I will do the scales, double thirds, and double sixths.

M: Why do you do Bach fugues?

B: They completely clear my mind and I feel fresh afterwards. I can be disturbed, troubled, and unhappy with the world in general, but a Bach fugue puts me back in order. There is a rightness about the music, and it's the greatest there is.

M: By the same token, don't you feel, when you're not in the mood for either playing a concert or making music, you may just sit down and play through a warm, beautiful piece of any kind?

B: To get myself in love with music again—I've very often done this. I remember once hearing Elisabeth Schwarzkopf in Texas. Before the concert, I went backstage, and knocked at her door. She answered, "Come in!" And I beheld her standing in front of the mirror, shaking her fist at herself. I said, "Madame Schwarzkopf, why are you doing that?" She replied, "I feel awful. I don't want to sing in twenty minutes, and I must make myself do it. I am forcing myself into that discipline." And she got out on stage and gave a fabulous performance!

M: That's wonderful; I understand perfectly. John, we have spoken so often about tone, and the quality of sound being produced today. I believe young people do what they feel more readily than they used to, but they do not listen to what they hear. What do you advise, in order to achieve deeper tone production?

B: I think what you just said is the clue. They listen to what they feel, and not to what they hear. Part of this can be learned from stage experience where you do not trust your ears, but you trust the outer ear that you develop, an ear which goes to the back of the hall and tells you what the sound is really like. The one major keyboard approach which disturbs me is the non-legato touch employed so much today. Any level of sound must have meaning. The legato must be especially deep and connected, because we are dealing with a non-legato instrument. The hand, arm, and wrist must, in fact, feel the pressure of depth in the key. Use a flat finger or a curved finger, I don't care which—but the depth must be there.

The modern instruments are becoming less and less good. We remember the pre-war pianos, which usually were good or great. We are now confronted with instruments which range from dreadful to great. When one is compelled to play on a piano with hammers that are steely and edgy, the worst thing one can do is to strike the key fast. The best thing one can do is to pull the sound out. I remember Josef and Rosina Lhevinne saying to both of us, "You must approach the piano like a lover, not like an enemy." Don't hit it; stroke it. Pull the sound out slowly, and with depth. The physical act of working forward toward yourself, and not against the instrument; pulling the sound from the instrument will produce a deeper singing tone.

M: I'm so glad to hear you say all these things, because one is never happier than when some of one's own ideas are upheld. One of my pet phrases has always been, "You don't push sound into the instrument, you draw sound out of it." The reason for this is that the sound is in the instrument, and the music is in you.

B: The sound is also in your ears; the sound you *want* to get out of the piano is in your ears. We are dealing with an elusive instrument, one which has no character of its own. A fiddle, a voice, those are all involved with the body. We are automatically more removed from our instrument than any other single performer. That is why we must find a very personal way of pulling out of the piano what it has in it, and we must hear with ears trained in voice, violin, flute, clarinet, and oboe, because there is no such thing as a piano sound. There is no natural piano sound; we create the sound.

M: Bravo, John! As you know, we give lectures, teach, and we say these things continually, but when statements like these come from concertizing artists of your caliber, perhaps young students will take heed. Playing the piano is not pushing down black and white keys; there is a tremendous craft which becomes one's own personal technique eventually, and ultimately relates to everything one wishes to express in music.

B: Finally, I think that it's not being in love with music that counts (although one must always be in love with music) but it is being taken over by the music instead of imposing yourself on the

*I remember once hearing Elisabeth Schwarzkopf in
Texas. Before the concert, I went backstage, and
knocked at her door. She answered, "Come in!" And
I beheld her standing in front of the mirror, shaking
her fist at herself. I said, "Madame Schwarzkopf,
why are you doing that?" She replied, "I feel awful.
I don't want to sing in twenty minutes, and I must
make myself do it. I am forcing myself into that
discipline. And she got out on stage and gave a
fabulous performance! . . . John Browning.*

music. The music, eventually, and with maturity, comes *into* you and you only become the purveyor of the music. You must, of course, add your own personality, but to add your personality before you *understand* the music is a youthful mistake. I heard a performance years ago of a very great conductor doing the *St. Matthew Passion* of Bach. I'm the first one to feel that Bach is a passionate composer, but there were so many gestures which seemed inappropriate for this particular work and composer. Debussy, to my taste, should not be extrovertedly displayed, in spite of the fact that he was a great womanizer, and seduced most of his friends' wives. He was a *tactile sensualist*: the color, feel, and stroke. Mozart, obviously, was the most balanced, because it's all there: the delicacy, the guts, the tremendous virility which so many people don't see or play in his music. Tremendous virility, but with absolute security; the security of a man who can do needlepoint and not have his virility threatened. Scriabin, who became addicted to morphine, was suddenly thrust into a sensual world that he probably hadn't as yet experienced. Every emotion varies in the projection of its essence with each composer. One must judge as an interpreter and as a performer what kind of emotion one attributes to each composer.

M: I feel very much as you do. Think of the breadth and depth of Brahms, with all the long phrases and rich sonorities. This was a man of great loneliness who explored the depths of his soul, but with a sensuous kind of warmth and intense passion. He always had a longing for something, whereas Mozart, I would say, was at least twenty-five years old when he was born. Therefore, his music emerged crystallized and fully mature.

I'd like to talk a bit about the pedal, because it is one of the most subtle attributes of the piano.

B: Most students pedal the way one drives a car: they simply put their foot on the accelerator. The more they press down on it, the faster they go. They do not understand pedal as an instrument of color and, as Lhevinne said, "the soul of the piano." Without the pedal, we have no piano. The pedal has so many depths. In playing Mozart, I almost never use full pedal, but I almost never use "no pedal." I use a small degree of pedal which keeps the sound alive, warm, and liquid, but does not interfere with the passagework.

M: Don't you feel that it is comparable to using a little bit of

An old trick of Horowitz's is accenting with pedal: you pick your foot up off the pedal and wham it down on the top climax. You give just a hint of breath in a heavy texture, which is vital, and then you use the pedal as an accent. . . . John Browning.

I rarely change fingerings; in fact, most of my scores are unfingered. Sometimes I'm sorry about that, because if I take up a work years after I played it, I regret not having marked down the fingerings. Where the music itself is concerned: if something isn't making sense to me, either from my brain, ears, or heart, then I review the score again, because I feel somehow I will get a clue from that. Something will tell me from the score. . . . John Browning.

vibrato on the violin instead of a lot; just enough to give substance to the sound?

B: Yes, because the piano sound without pedal can be very boring.

M: It's as dry as oatmeal, unless you want it really *sec* and crisp. I'm always amazed when a pianist sees staccati notes and, because his musical understanding is minimal, never touches the pedal.

B: An old trick of Horowitz's which we both know is accenting with pedal: you pick your foot up off the pedal and wham it down on the top climax. You give just a hint of breath in a heavy texture, which is vital, and then you use the pedal as an accent.

M: And when you are playing a passage of running notes which requires a brilliant phrase accentuation, you can snap off the pedal sharply for the necessary effect. The pedal is a pianist's life-long aid, which we must guard carefully.

B: If we take Josef Lhevinne's statement: "The pedal is the soul of the piano," one step further, we must think as intensively about the pedal as we would about our spiritual life. Not too many young people do, which is unfortunate.

M: I suggest that we all give courses on the pedal!

B: I remember, Adele, that you made a remark to me once about octaves: that you play Liszt octaves and Brahms octaves totally differently. The Liszt octaves must be played brilliantly, with pointed fingers and strong wrists; the Brahms octaves must be heavy and shoulderish. The same is true with pedal. Pedaling must change from composer to composer. Students tend to pedal by formula; they don't use their ears or imaginations when they pedal.

M: Most students, in my experience, isolate pedaling from the actual music making: "Is it too long, is it too short, where do I put it down?" and so on. The music absolutely dictates to us what we must do.

B: Pedaling is emotional; this is what I think is important to realize. Pedaling is not exclusively mechanical. It has nothing to do with putting one's foot down every so often. It is an emotional act, and it's intuitive— like holding hands with someone.

M: How do you feel about the pedal in playing Bach?

B: Give the sound just enough liquid quality so that it isn't dry or boring. The harpsichord with its less effective dampers produced an overhang which doesn't exist on the piano. For the piano, one must use just enough pedal to keep the texture and color warm, but not so much as to obscure the articulation. Of course, the standard rule is that any figuration in the bass must be cleared much faster than anything in the treble. But by the same token, you can hold bass notes at half pedal and keep them, while clearing the upper register. But this is an art in itself; it must never be thought of as anything other than an art. It all takes very careful handling.

M: I am sure that you bring these things into focus whenever you give master classes. It is an invaluable contribution. More people ought to take time with all aspects of playing the instrument in order to make music.

B: We could go on forever!

M: Isn't it fascinating, though, the great art that it is? When people ask me, "How can you teach Op. 109, 110 and 111 again and again?" I say to them, "It's never the same; it's never the same piece." There is always the spontaneous reaction and newness of its great magic. Thank you for being so lucid and beautifully specific, John. It felt like old times!